Alfred's Basic Piano Library
ELEMENTARY MUSICIANSHIP

Willard A. Palmer • Morton Manus • Amanda Vick Lethco

Book One

© Copyright MCMLXXXVII by Alfred Publishing Co., Inc.
All rights reserved.   Printed in USA.

Foreword

This book is an important resource for piano students, including those preparing for National Guild Auditions. It may be used with Alfred's Basic Piano Library as early as Level 1B for students playing tetrachord scales divided between the hands. It is equally useful with other method books.

Technical ease in playing scales and chords is logically developed through a presentation of all the major and minor scales, arpeggios, and I V I and I V7 I cadences in each key. Study of these materials will also develop sight reading and memory skills because of a more complete awareness of the component parts of music. Pieces then become easier to play. Individual scales and chords should be assigned in the keys of all pieces being studied; other keys may be added as the teacher wishes.

The Enrichment Options, beginning on page 35, are designed to further develop musicianship. They suggest a number of additional ways the scales and chords in the first section may be played. Some of the options should be practiced in every key being studied. It is the hope of the authors that each student who uses this Elementary Musicianship Book will have greater freedom at the keyboard and more pleasure in making music.

Willard A. Palmer • Morton Manus • Amanda Vick Lethco

Contents

C MAJOR and C MINOR	Scales and Triads	4
	Arpeggios and Cadences	5
G MAJOR and G MINOR	Scales and Triads	6
	Arpeggios and Cadences	7
D MAJOR and D MINOR	Scales and Triads	8
	Arpeggios and Cadences	9
A MAJOR and A MINOR	Scales and Triads	10
	Arpeggios and Cadences	11
E MAJOR and E MINOR	Scales and Triads	12
	Arpeggios and Cadences	13
B MAJOR and B MINOR	Scales and Triads	14
	Arpeggios and Cadences	15
C♭ MAJOR and C♭ MINOR	Scales and Triads	16
	Arpeggios and Cadences	17
F♯ MAJOR and F♯ MINOR	Scales and Triads	18
	Arpeggios and Cadences	19
G♭ MAJOR and G♭ MINOR	Scales and Triads	20
	Arpeggios and Cadences	21
C♯ MAJOR and C♯ MINOR	Scales and Triads	22
	Arpeggios and Cadences	23
D♭ MAJOR and D♭ MINOR	Scales and Triads	24
	Arpeggios and Cadences	25
A♭ MAJOR and G♯ MINOR	Scales and Triads	26
	Arpeggios and Cadences	27
E♭ MAJOR and E♭ MINOR	Scales and Triads	28
	Arpeggios and Cadences	29
B♭ MAJOR and B♭ MINOR	Scales and Triads	30
	Arpeggios and Cadences	31
F MAJOR and F MINOR	Scales and Triads	32
	Arpeggios and Cadences	33

MAJOR KEYS, MINOR KEYS & KEY SIGNATURES Around the Circle of 5ths ..34

ENRICHMENT OPTIONS
    Cadences 35
    Scales 35
    Triad Chain 37
    Dominant 7th Chord Resolving to Its Major Tonic Chord 38
    Dominant 7th Chord Resolving to Its Minor Tonic Chord 40

SCALES—THE GRAND FORM 42

MAJOR SCALES, 2 OCTAVES 43

HARMONIC MINOR SCALES, 2 OCTAVES 46

C MAJOR and C MINOR — Scales & Triads

C MAJOR SCALE in TETRACHORDS
Key Signature: No sharps, no flats.

C MAJOR SCALE, ONE OCTAVE, hands separately or together

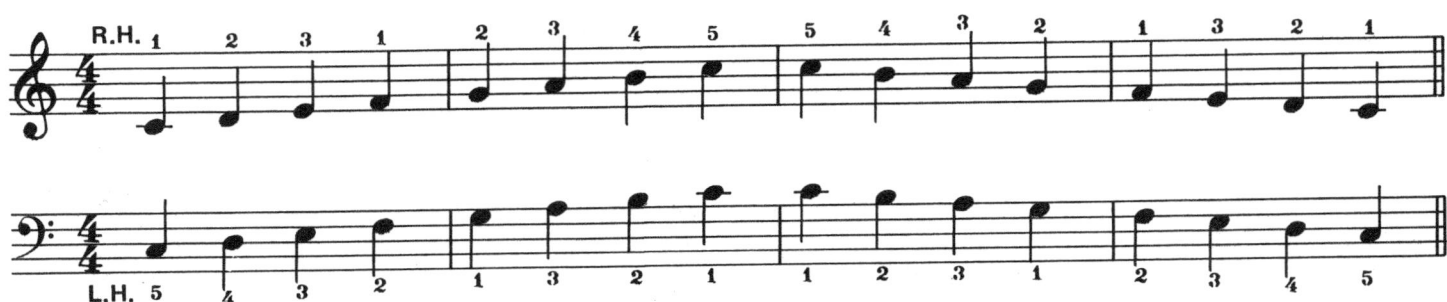

For the two-octave scale, see page 43.

C HARMONIC MINOR SCALE, hands separately or together

C Minor is the Relative Minor of E♭ MAJOR. Key Signature: 3 flats (B♭, E♭ & A♭).
The 7th scale tone (B♭) is raised one half-step ascending and descending.

For the two-octave scale, see page 46.

TRIADS in 3 POSITIONS, hands separately or together

C MAJOR TRIAD — C MINOR TRIAD

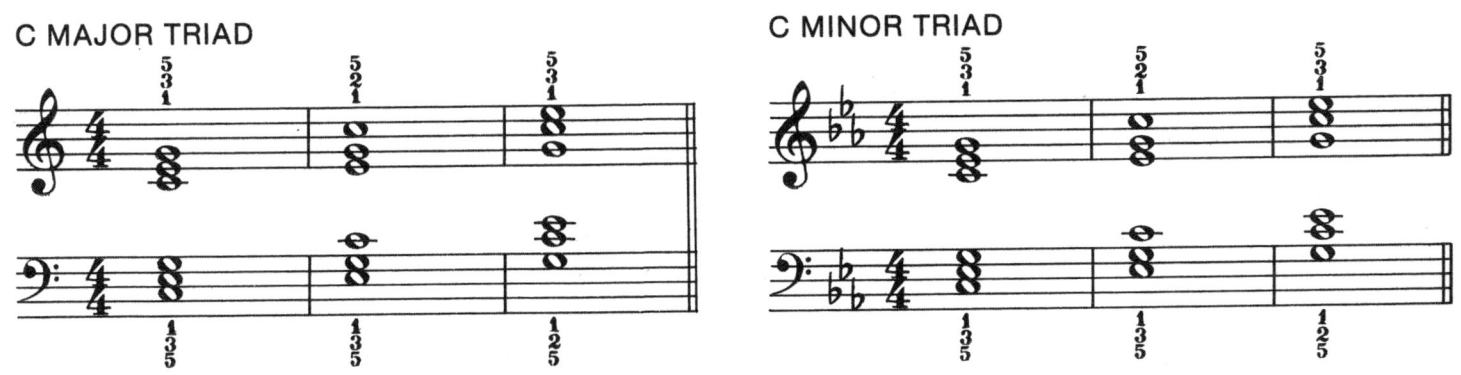

Arpeggios & Cadences

C MAJOR ARPEGGIO

2nd time BOTH HANDS 2 octaves higher

C MINOR ARPEGGIO

2nd time BOTH HANDS 2 octaves higher

C MAJOR ARPEGGIO, with thumb turns

C MINOR ARPEGGIO, with thumb turns

C MAJOR CADENCES, hands separately or together

C MINOR CADENCES, hands separately or together

G MAJOR and G MINOR — Scales & Triads

G MAJOR SCALE in TETRACHORDS
Key Signature: 1 sharp (F♯).

G MAJOR SCALE, ONE OCTAVE, hands separately or together

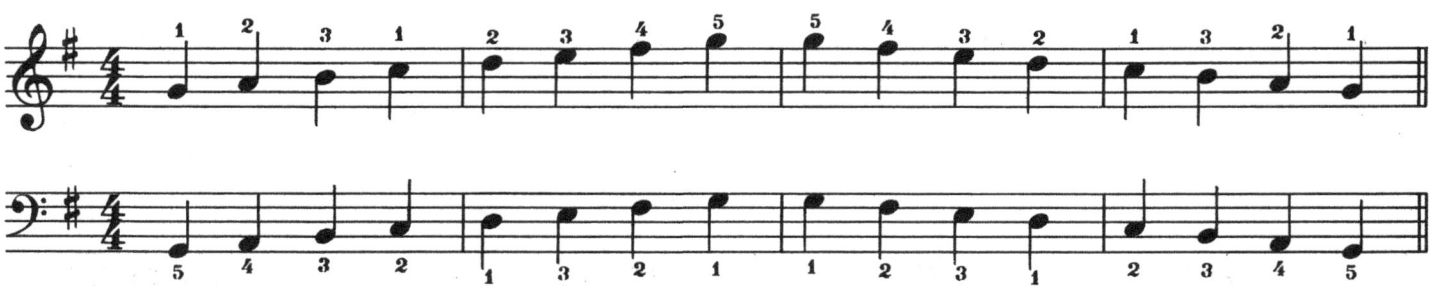

For the two-octave scale, see page 43.

G HARMONIC MINOR SCALE, hands separately or together
G Minor is the Relative Minor of B♭ MAJOR. Key Signature: 2 flats (B♭ & E♭).
The 7th scale tone (F) is raised one half-step ascending and descending.

For the two-octave scale, see page 46.

TRIADS in 3 POSITIONS, hands separately or together
G MAJOR TRIAD   G MINOR TRIAD

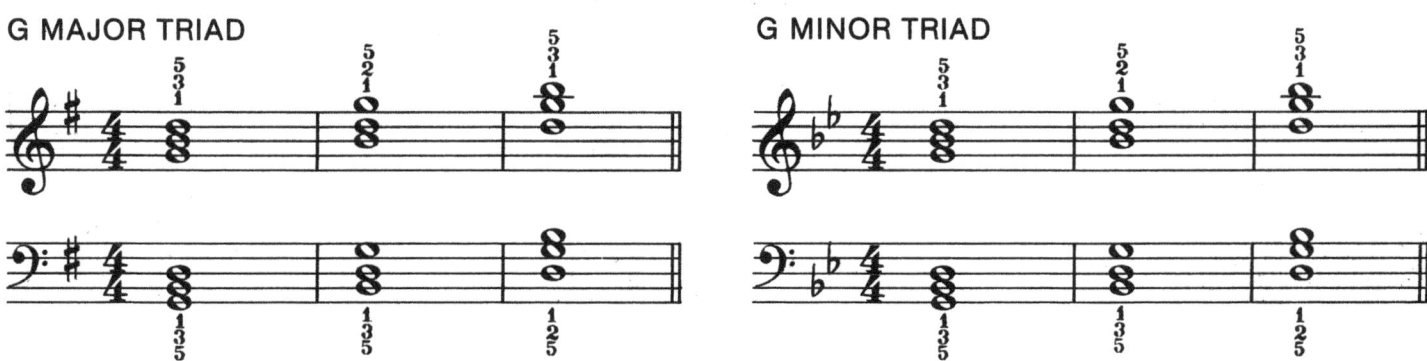

Arpeggios & Cadences

G MAJOR ARPEGGIO
2nd time BOTH HANDS 2 octaves higher

G MINOR ARPEGGIO
2nd time BOTH HANDS 2 octaves higher

G MAJOR ARPEGGIO, with thumb turns

G MINOR ARPEGGIO, with thumb turns

G MAJOR CADENCES, hands separately or together

G MINOR CADENCES, hands separately or together

D MAJOR and D MINOR — Scales & Triads

D MAJOR SCALE in TETRACHORDS
Key Signature: 2 sharps (F♯ & C♯).

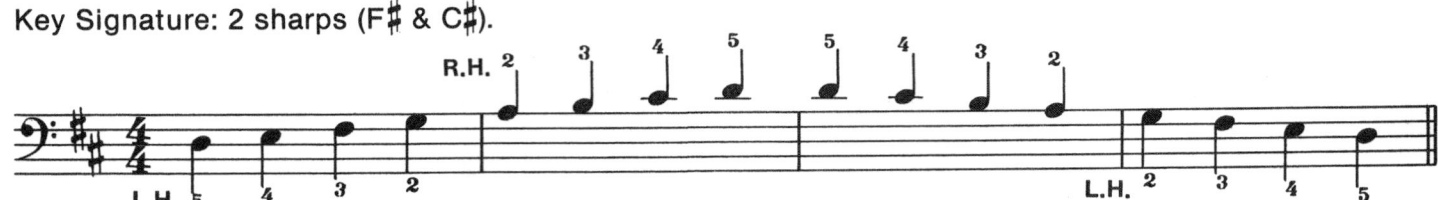

D MAJOR SCALE, ONE OCTAVE, hands separately or together

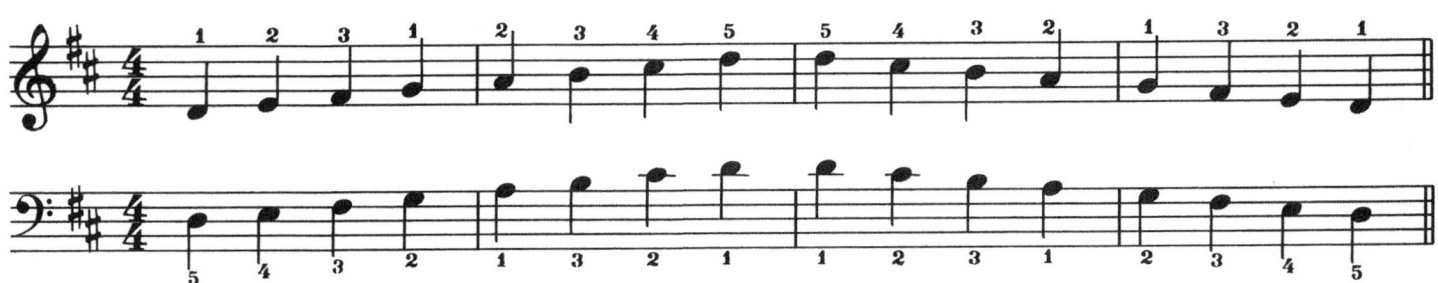

For the two-octave scale, see page 43.

D HARMONIC MINOR SCALE, hands separately or together
D Minor is the Relative Minor of F MAJOR. Key Signature: 1 flat (B♭).
The 7th scale tone (C) is raised one half-step ascending and descending.

For the two-octave scale, see page 46.

TRIADS in 3 POSITIONS, hands separately or together

D MAJOR TRIAD   D MINOR TRIAD

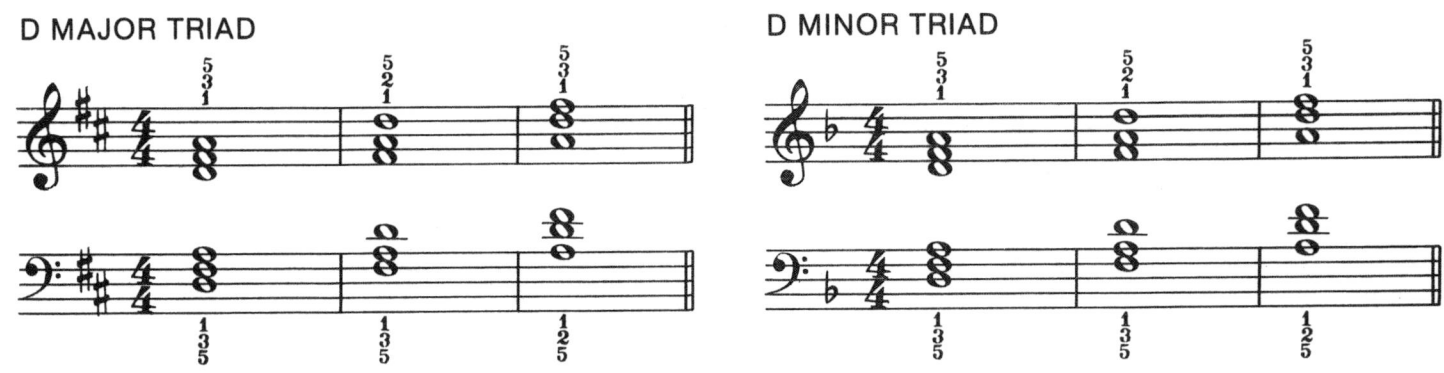

Arpeggios & Cadences

D MAJOR ARPEGGIO
2nd time BOTH HANDS 2 octaves higher

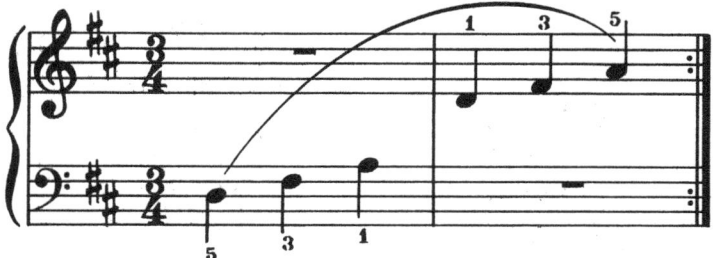

D MINOR ARPEGGIO
2nd time BOTH HANDS 2 octaves higher

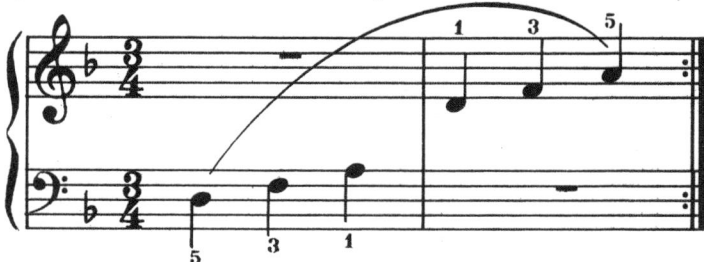

D MAJOR ARPEGGIO, with thumb turns

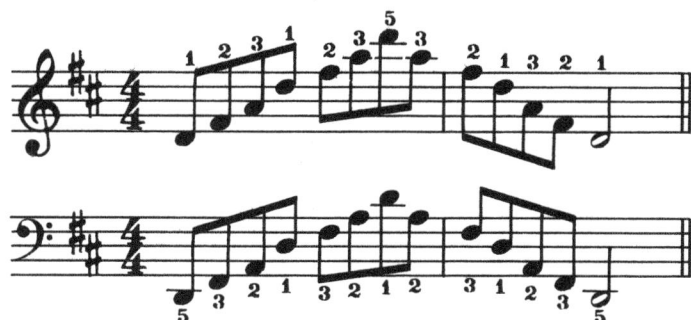

D MINOR ARPEGGIO, with thumb turns

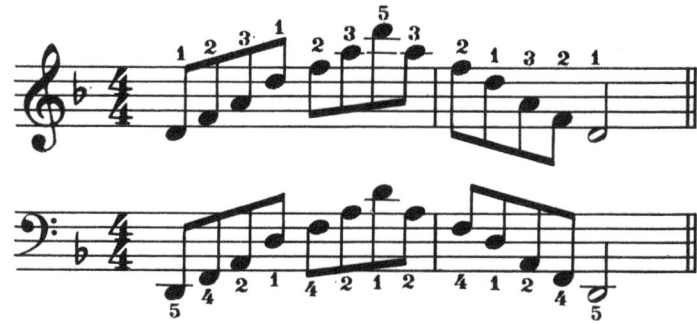

D MAJOR CADENCES, hands separately or together

D MINOR CADENCES, hands separately or together

A MAJOR and A MINOR   Scales & Triads

A MAJOR SCALE in TETRACHORDS
Key Signature: 3 sharps (F#, C# & G#).

A MAJOR SCALE, ONE OCTAVE, hands separately or together

For the two-octave scale, see page 43.

A HARMONIC MINOR SCALE, hands separately or together

A Minor is the Relative Minor of C MAJOR. Key Signature: no sharps, no flats.
The 7th scale tone (G) is raised one half-step ascending and descending.

For the two-octave scale, see page 46.

TRIADS in 3 POSITIONS, hands separately or together

A MAJOR TRIAD   A MINOR TRIAD

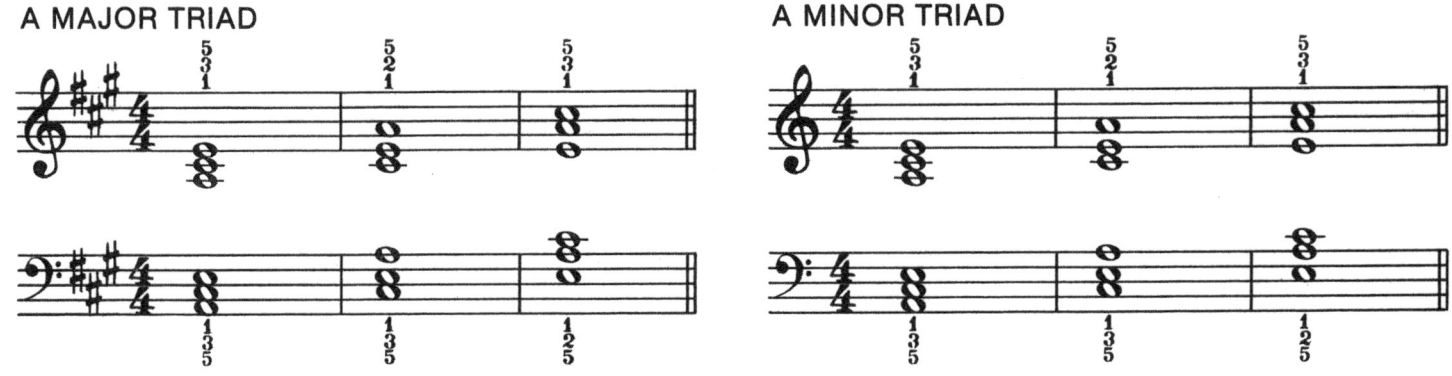

Arpeggios & Cadences

A MAJOR ARPEGGIO
2nd time BOTH HANDS 2 octaves higher

A MINOR ARPEGGIO
2nd time BOTH HANDS 2 octaves higher

A MAJOR ARPEGGIO, with thumb turns

A MINOR ARPEGGIO, with thumb turns

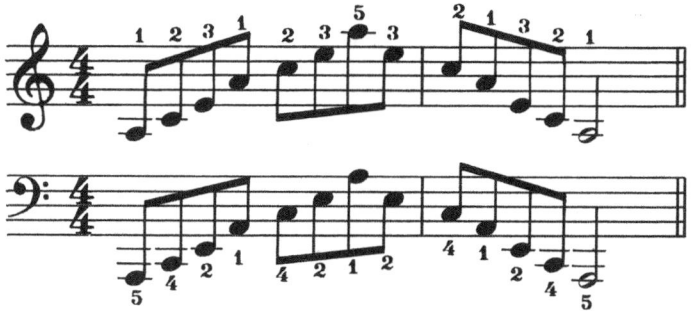

A MAJOR CADENCES, hands separately or together

A MINOR CADENCES, hands separately or together

E MAJOR and E MINOR — Scales & Triads

E MAJOR SCALE in TETRACHORDS
Key Signature: 4 sharps (F♯, C♯, G♯ & D♯).

E MAJOR SCALE, ONE OCTAVE, hands separately or together

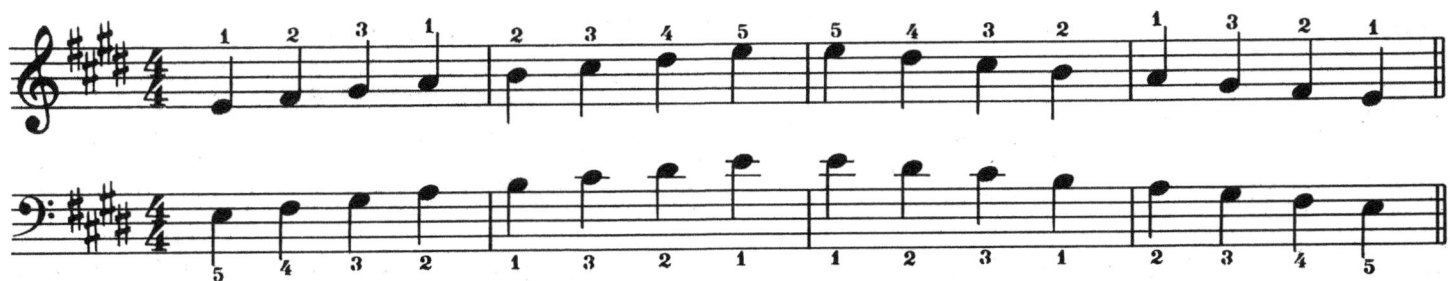

For the two-octave scale, see page 43.

E HARMONIC MINOR SCALE, hands separately or together

E Minor is the Relative Minor of G MAJOR. Key Signature: 1 sharp (F♯).
The 7th scale tone (D) is raised one half-step ascending and descending.

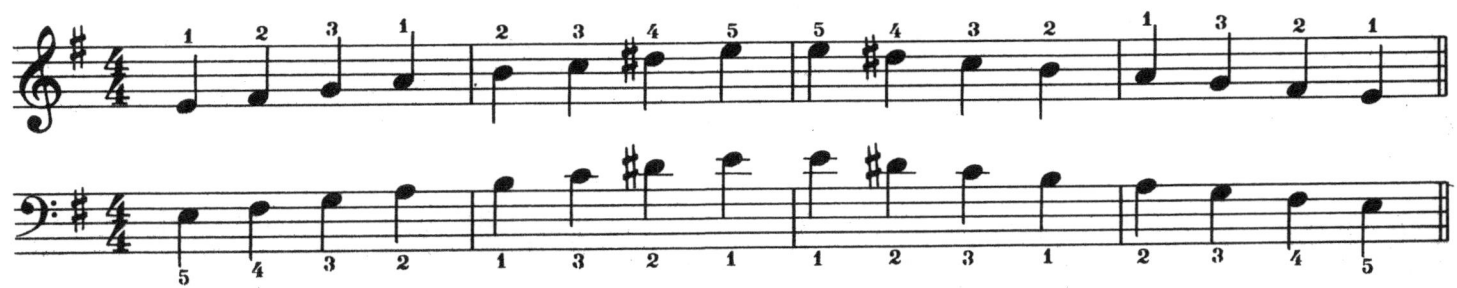

For the two-octave scale, see page 47.

TRIADS in 3 POSITIONS, hands separately or together

E MAJOR TRIAD   E MINOR TRIAD

Arpeggios & Cadences

E MAJOR ARPEGGIO

2nd time BOTH HANDS 2 octaves higher

E MINOR ARPEGGIO

2nd time BOTH HANDS 2 octaves higher

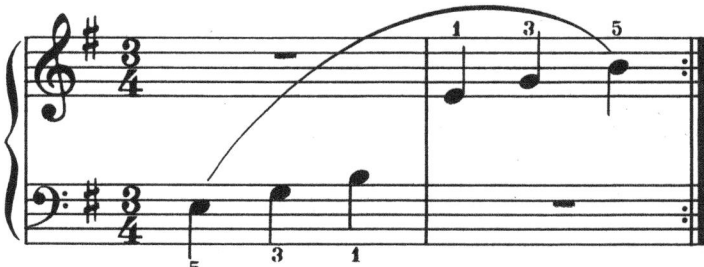

E MAJOR ARPEGGIO, with thumb turns

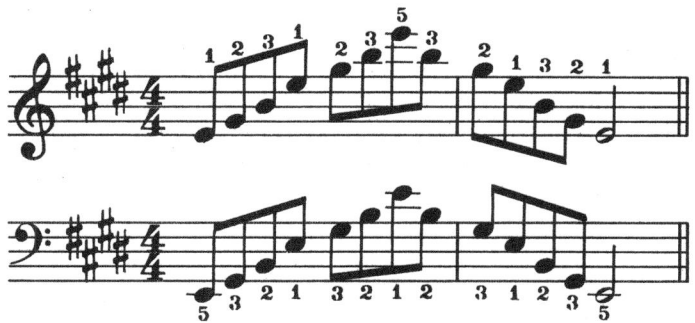

E MINOR ARPEGGIO, with thumb turns

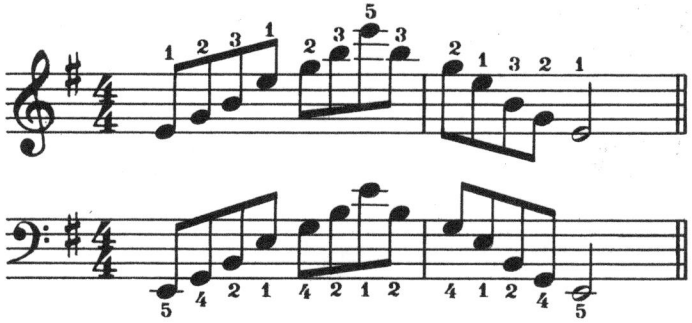

E MAJOR CADENCES, hands separately or together

E MINOR CADENCES, hands separately or together

B MAJOR and B MINOR — Scales & Triads

B MAJOR SCALE in TETRACHORDS
Key Signature: 5 sharps (F♯, C♯, G♯, D♯ & A♯).

B MAJOR SCALE, ONE OCTAVE, hands separately or together

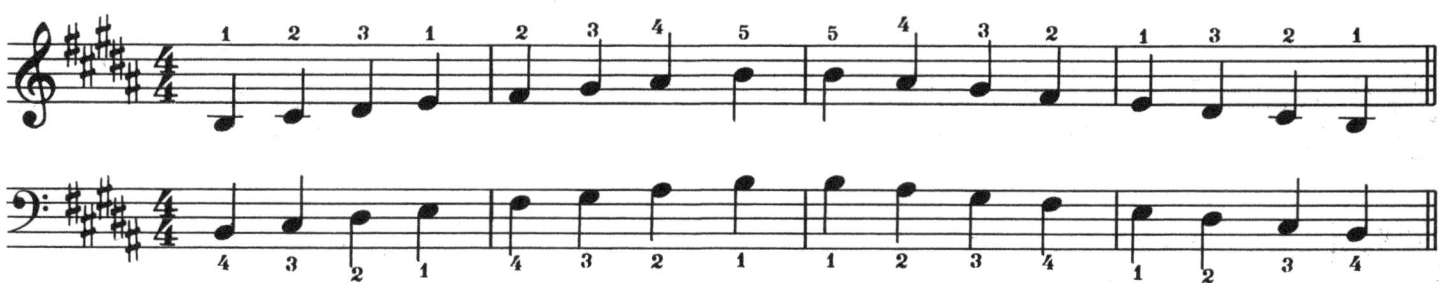

For the two-octave scale, see page 44.

B HARMONIC MINOR SCALE, hands separately or together
B Minor is the Relative Minor of D MAJOR. Key Signature: 2 sharps (F♯ & C♯).
The 7th scale tone (A) is raised one half-step ascending and descending.

For the two-octave scale, see page 47.

TRIADS in 3 POSITIONS, hands separately or together

B MAJOR TRIAD   B MINOR TRIAD

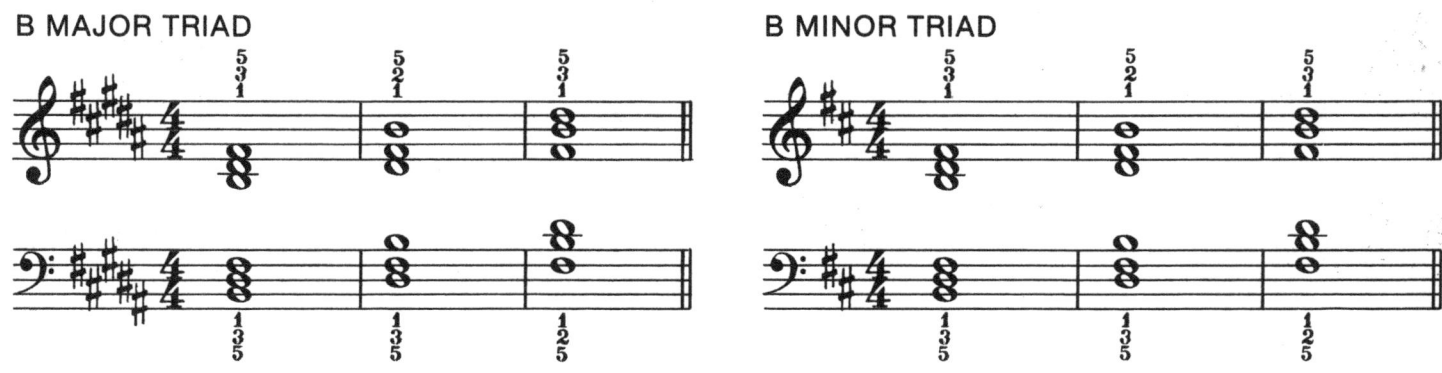

Arpeggios & Cadences

B MAJOR ARPEGGIO

2nd time BOTH HANDS 2 octaves higher

B MINOR ARPEGGIO

2nd time BOTH HANDS 2 octaves higher

B MAJOR ARPEGGIO, with thumb turns

B MINOR ARPEGGIO, with thumb turns

B MAJOR CADENCES, hands separately or together

B MINOR CADENCES, hands separately or together

C♭ MAJOR and C♭ MINOR
Enharmonic with B

Scales & Triads

C♭ MAJOR SCALE in TETRACHORDS
Key Signature: 7 flats (B♭, E♭, A♭, D♭, G♭, C♭, F♭)

C♭ MAJOR SCALE, ONE OCTAVE, hands separately or together

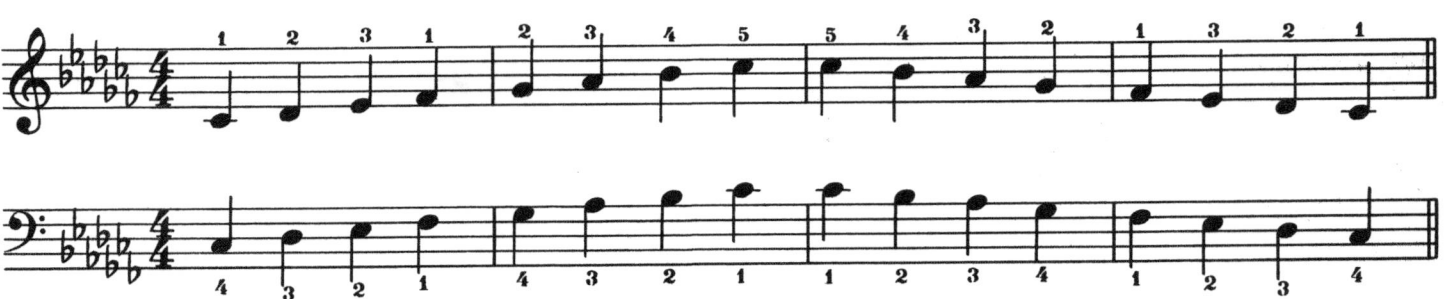

For the two-octave scale, see page 44.

TRIADS in 3 POSITIONS, hands separately or together
C♭ MAJOR TRIAD

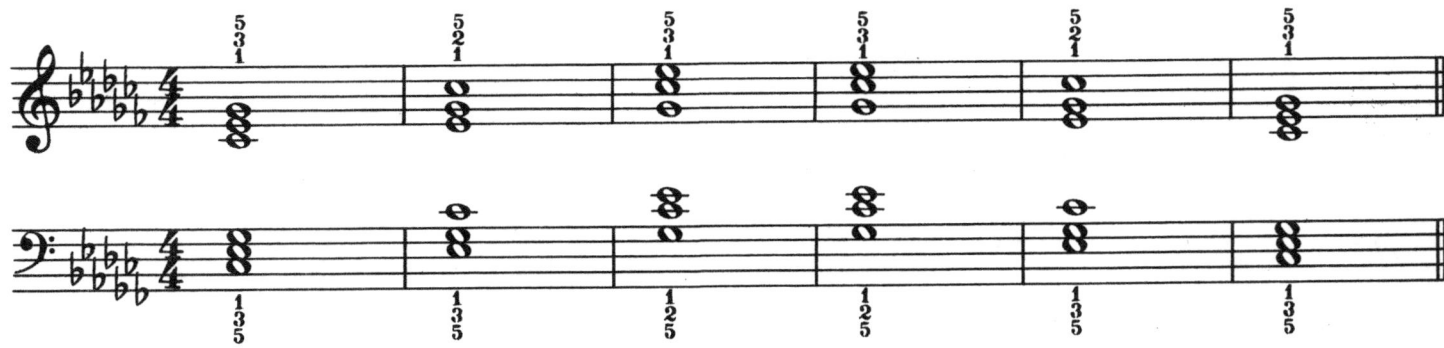

Arpeggios & Cadences

C♭ MAJOR ARPEGGIO

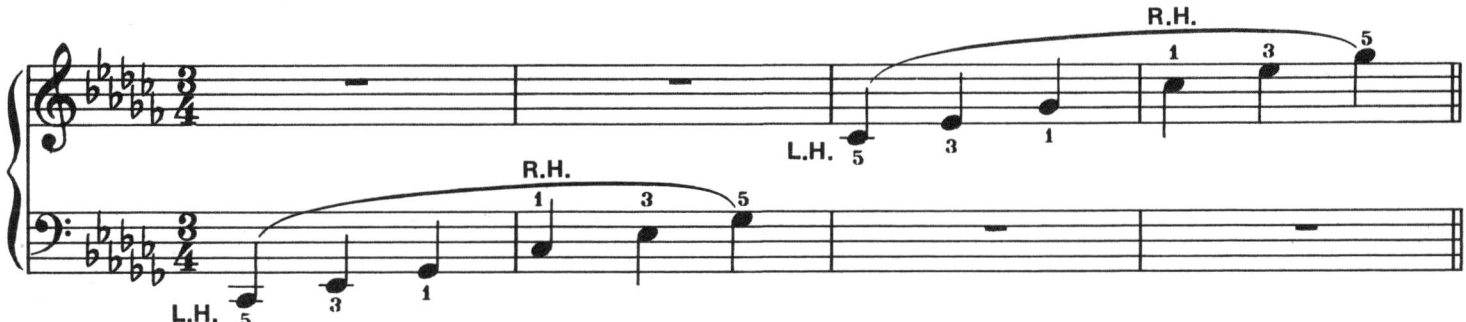

C♭ MINOR is enharmonic with B minor. See B minor arpeggios on page 15.

C♭ MAJOR ARPEGGIO, with thumb turns

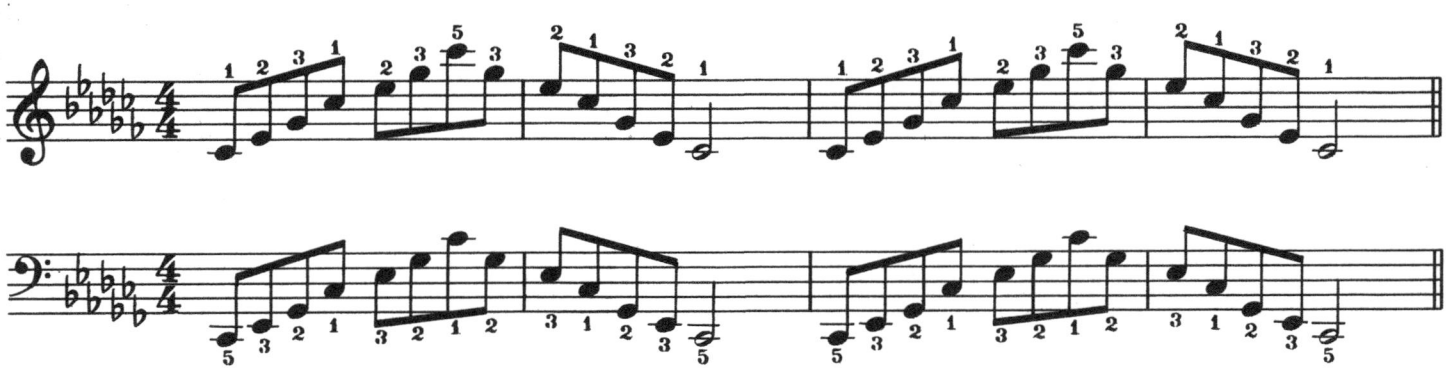

C♭ MAJOR CADENCES, hands separately or together

C♭ MINOR CADENCES (See B minor cadences on page 15.)

F# MAJOR and F# MINOR — Scales & Triads

F# MAJOR SCALE in TETRACHORDS
Key Signature: 6 sharps (F#, C#, G#, D#, A# & E#).

F# MAJOR SCALE, ONE OCTAVE, hands separately or together

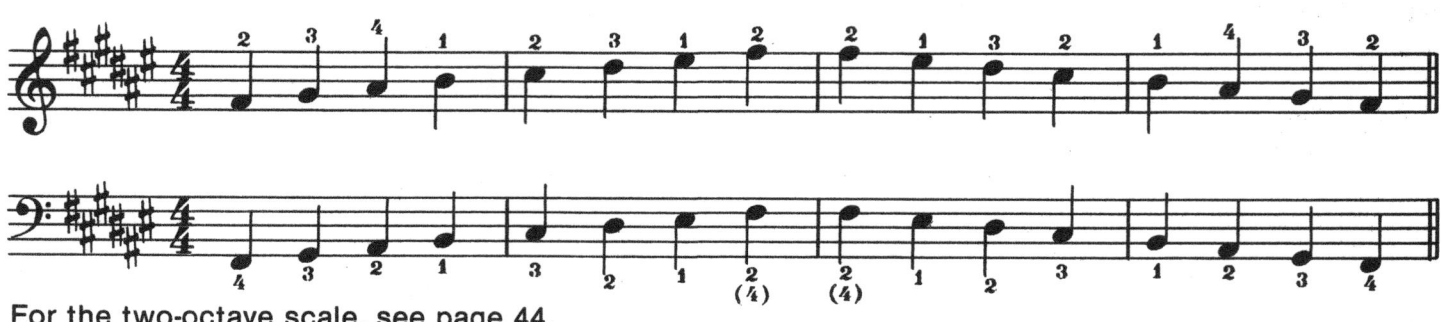

For the two-octave scale, see page 44.

F# HARMONIC MINOR SCALE, hands separately or together
F# Minor is the Relative Minor of A MAJOR. Key Signature: 3 sharps (F#, C# & G#).
The 7th scale tone (E) is raised one half-step ascending and descending.

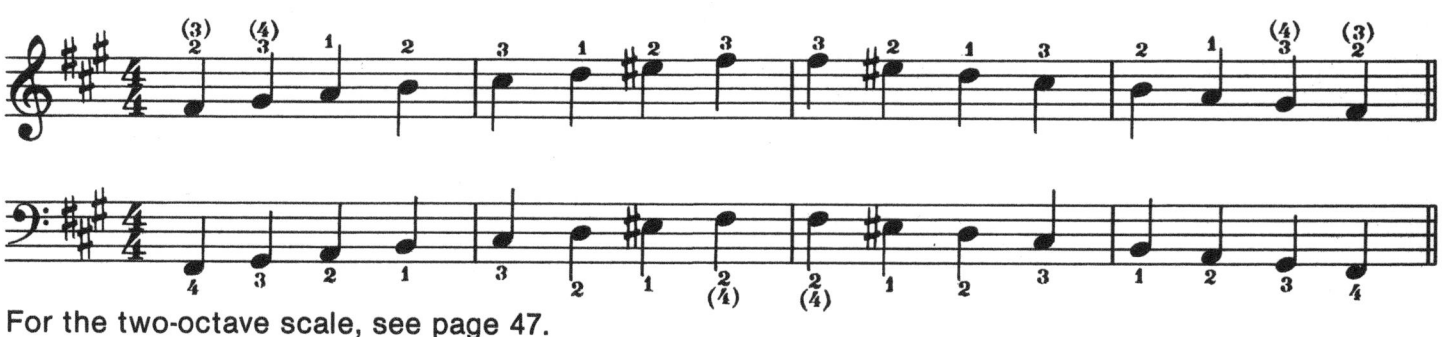

For the two-octave scale, see page 47.

TRIADS in 3 POSITIONS, hands separately or together

F# MAJOR TRIAD   F# MINOR TRIAD

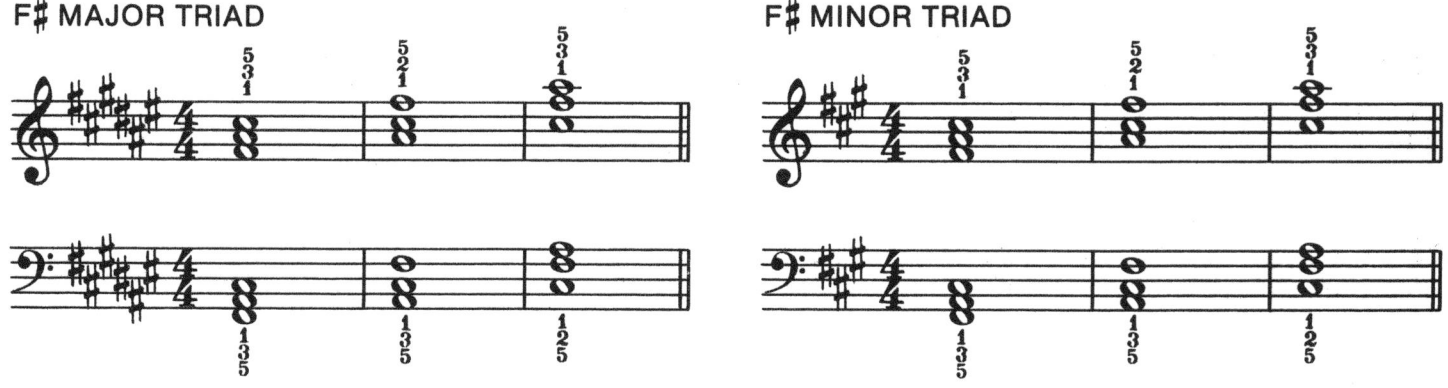

Arpeggios & Cadences

F# MAJOR ARPEGGIO

2nd time BOTH HANDS 2 octaves higher

F# MINOR ARPEGGIO

2nd time BOTH HANDS 2 octaves higher

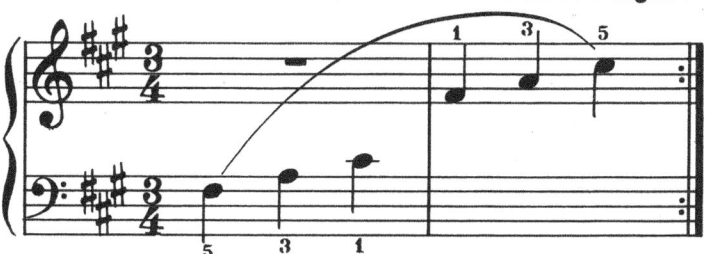

F# MAJOR ARPEGGIO, with thumb turns

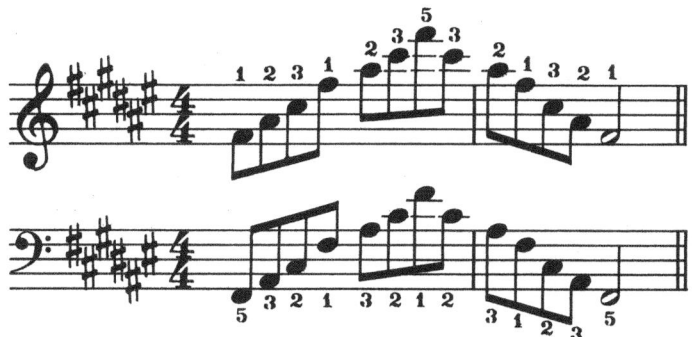

F# MINOR ARPEGGIO, with thumb turns

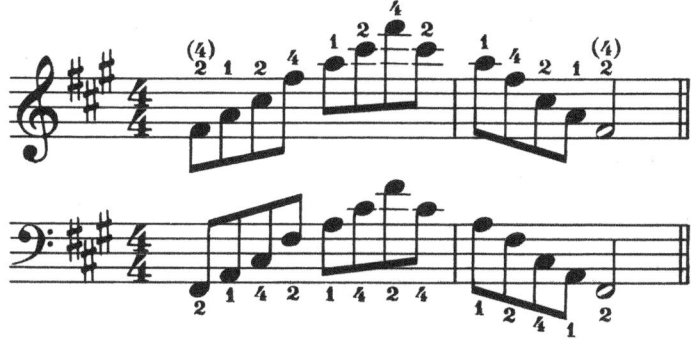

F# MAJOR CADENCES, hands separately or together

F# MINOR CADENCES, hands separately or together

G♭ MAJOR and G♭ MINOR
Enharmonic with F♯

Scales & Triads

G♭ MAJOR SCALE in TETRACHORDS
Key Signature: 6 flats (B♭, E♭, A♭, D♭, G♭ & C♭).

G♭ MAJOR SCALE, ONE OCTAVE, hands separately or together

For the two-octave scale, see page 44.

TRIADS in 3 POSITIONS, hands separately or together
G♭ MAJOR TRIAD

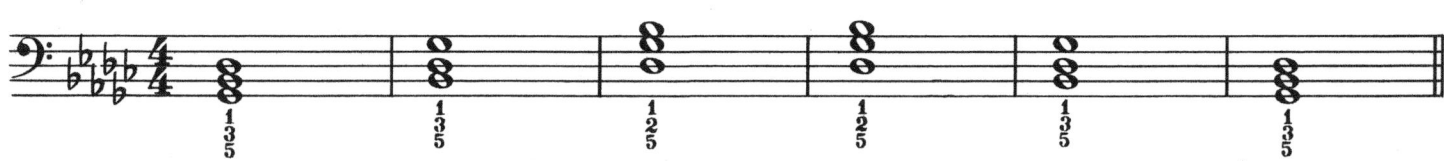

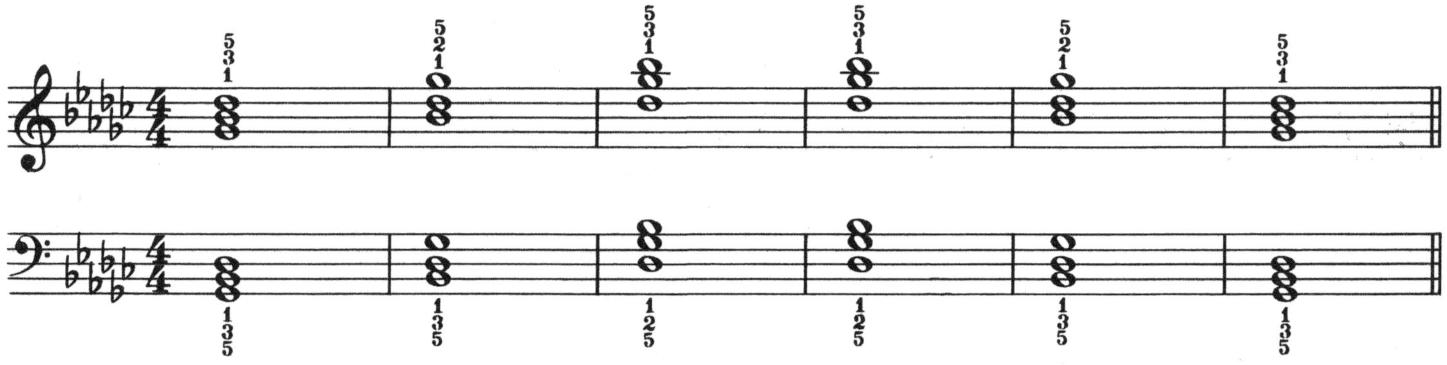

Arpeggios & Cadences

G♭ MAJOR ARPEGGIO

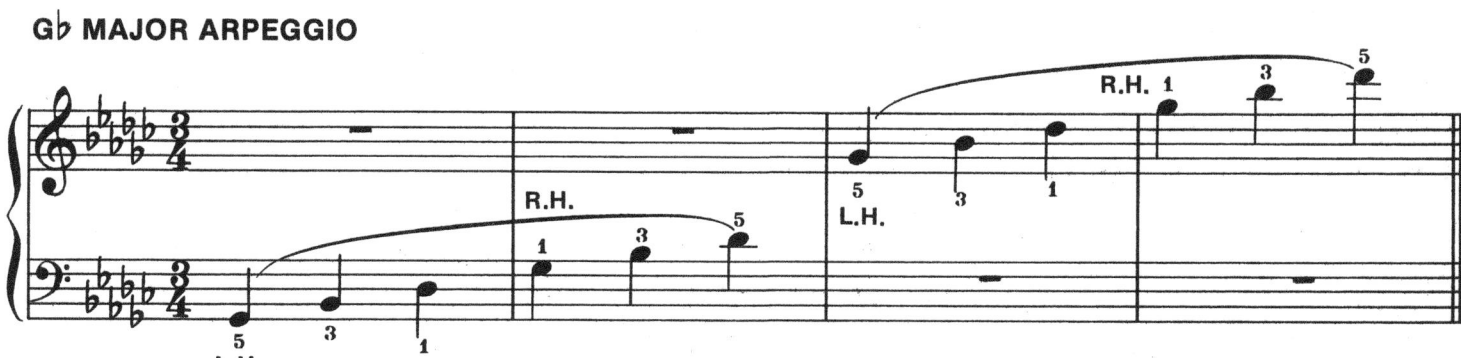

G♭ MINOR is enharmonic with F♯ minor. See F♯ minor arpeggios on page 19.

G♭ MAJOR ARPEGGIO, with thumb turns

G♭ MAJOR CADENCES, hands separately or together

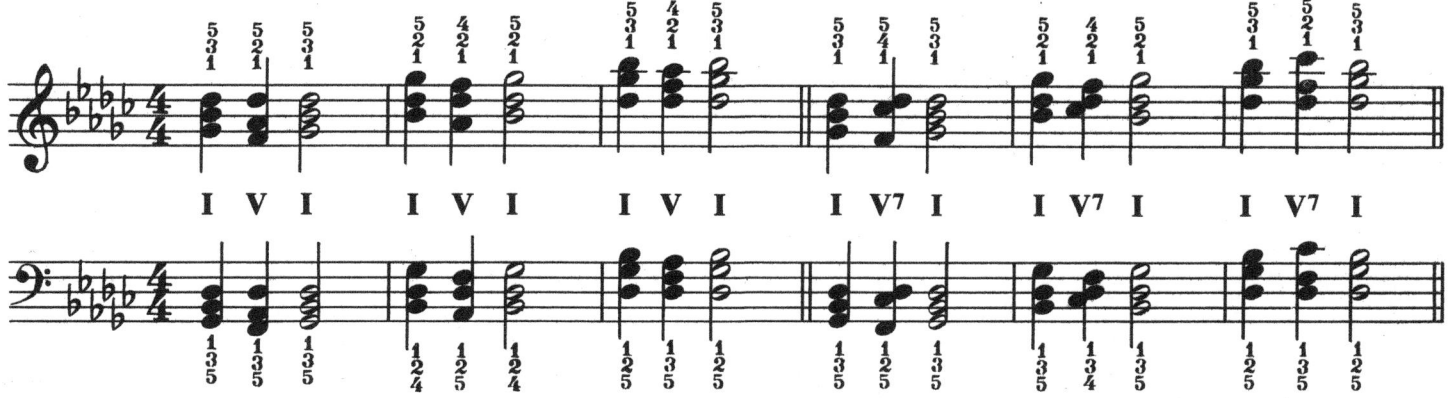

G♭ MINOR CADENCES (See F♯ minor cadences on page 19.)

C♯ MAJOR and C♯ MINOR — Scales & Triads

C♯ MAJOR SCALE in TETRACHORDS
Key Signature: 7 sharps (F♯, C♯, G♯, D♯, A♯, E♯ & B♯).

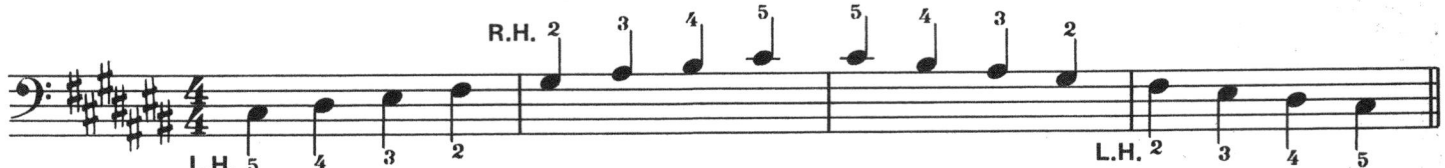

C♯ MAJOR SCALE, ONE OCTAVE, hands separately or together

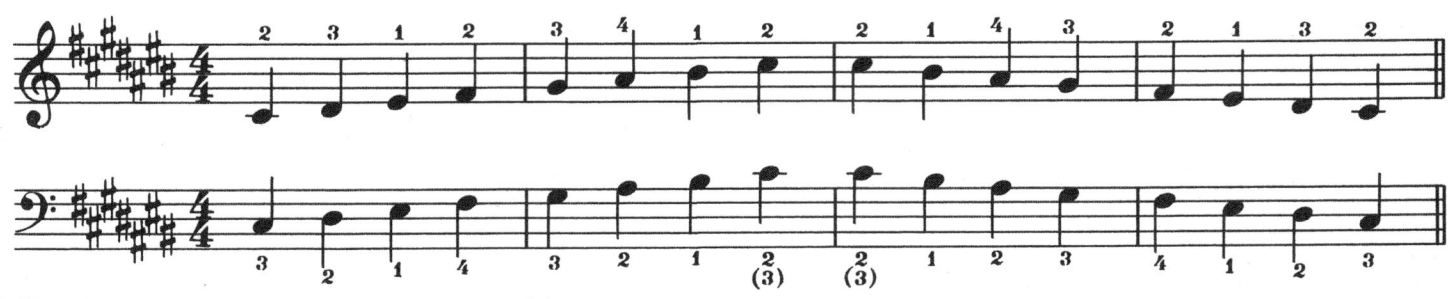

For the two-octave scale, see page 44.

C♯ HARMONIC MINOR SCALE, hands separately or together
C♯ Minor is the Relative Minor of E MAJOR. Key Signature: 4 sharps (F♯, C♯, G♯ & D♯).
The 7th scale tone (B) is raised one half-step ascending and descending.

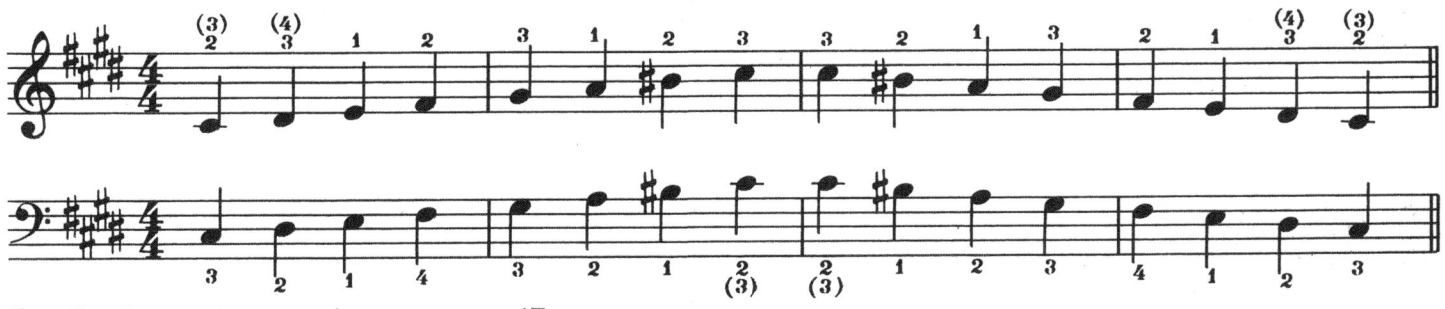

For the two-octave scale, see page 47.

TRIADS in 3 POSITIONS, hands separately or together

C♯ MAJOR TRIAD   C♯ MINOR TRIAD

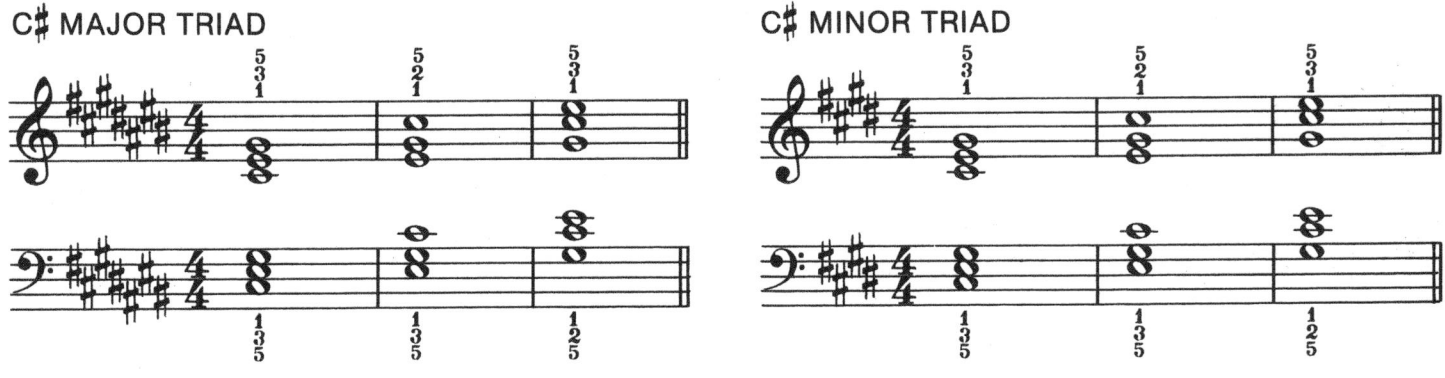

Arpeggios & Cadences

C# MAJOR ARPEGGIO
2nd time BOTH HANDS 2 octaves higher

C# MINOR ARPEGGIO
2nd time BOTH HANDS 2 octaves higher

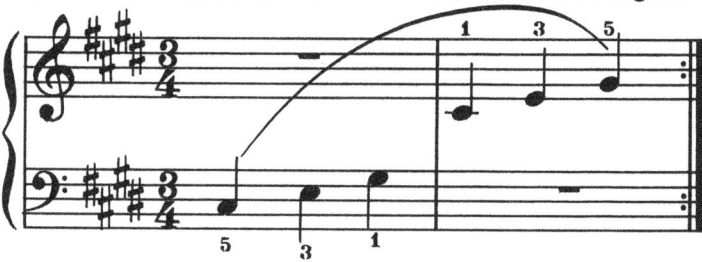

C# MAJOR ARPEGGIO, with thumb turns

C# MINOR ARPEGGIO, with thumb turns

C# MAJOR CADENCES, hands separately or together

C# MINOR CADENCES, hands separately or together

D♭ MAJOR and D♭ MINOR
Enharmonic with C♯

Scales & Triads

D♭ MAJOR SCALE in TETRACHORDS
Key Signature: 5 flats (B♭, E♭, A♭, D♭ & G♭).

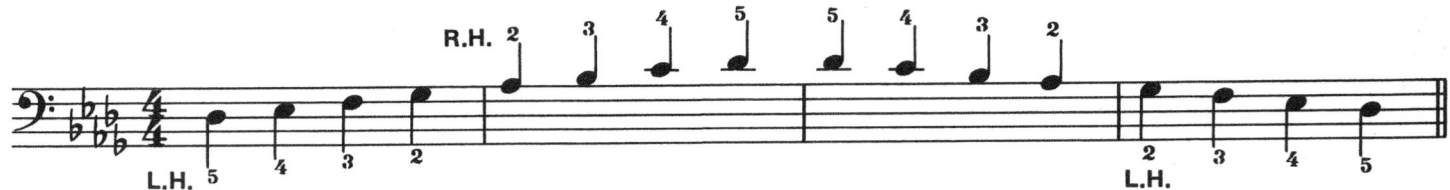

D♭ MAJOR SCALE, ONE OCTAVE, hands separately or together

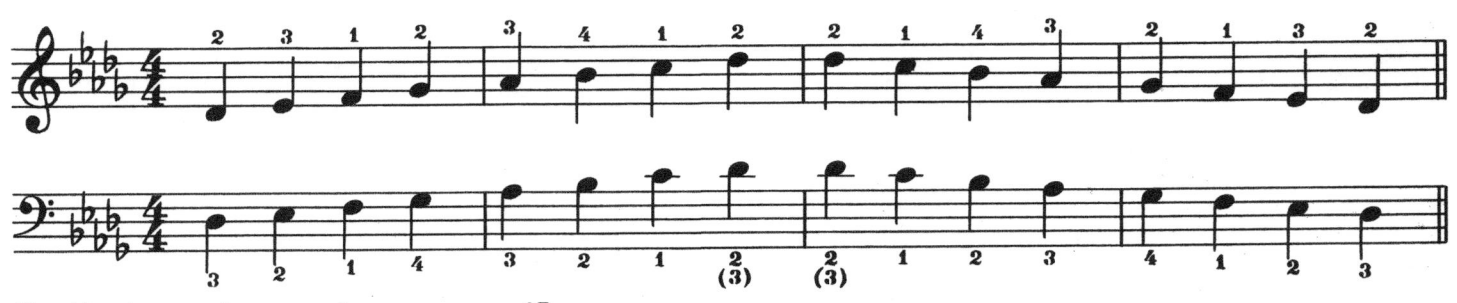

For the two-octave scale, see page 45.

TRIADS in 3 POSITIONS, hands separately or together
D♭ MAJOR TRIAD

Arpeggios & Cadences

D♭ MAJOR ARPEGGIO

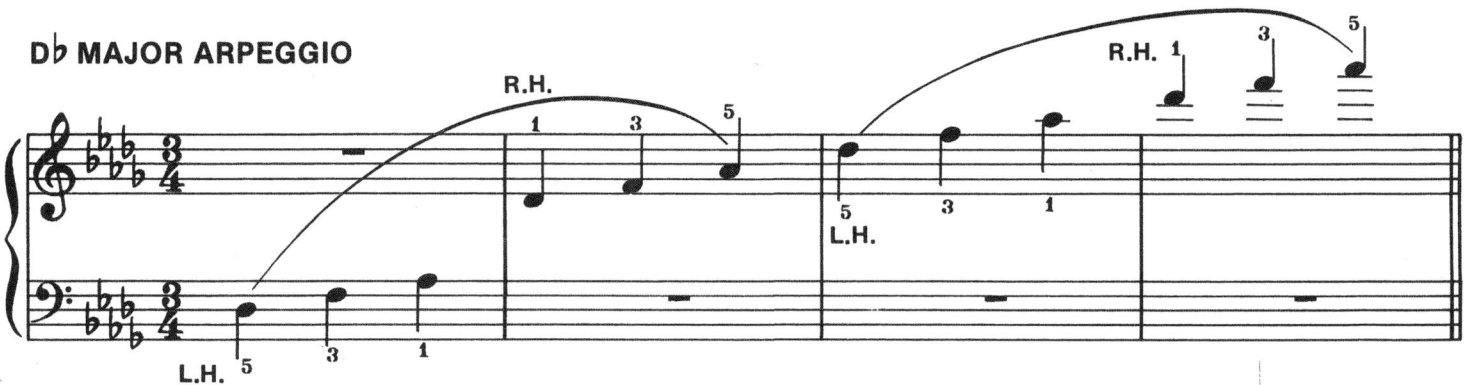

D♭ MINOR is enharmonic with C♯ minor. See C♯ minor arpeggios on page 23.

D♭ MAJOR ARPEGGIO, with thumb turns

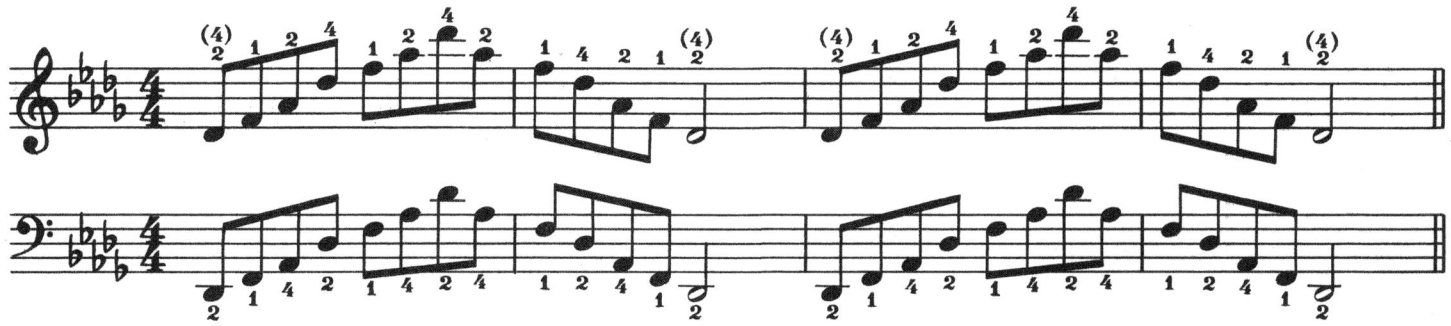

D♭ MAJOR CADENCES, hands separately or together

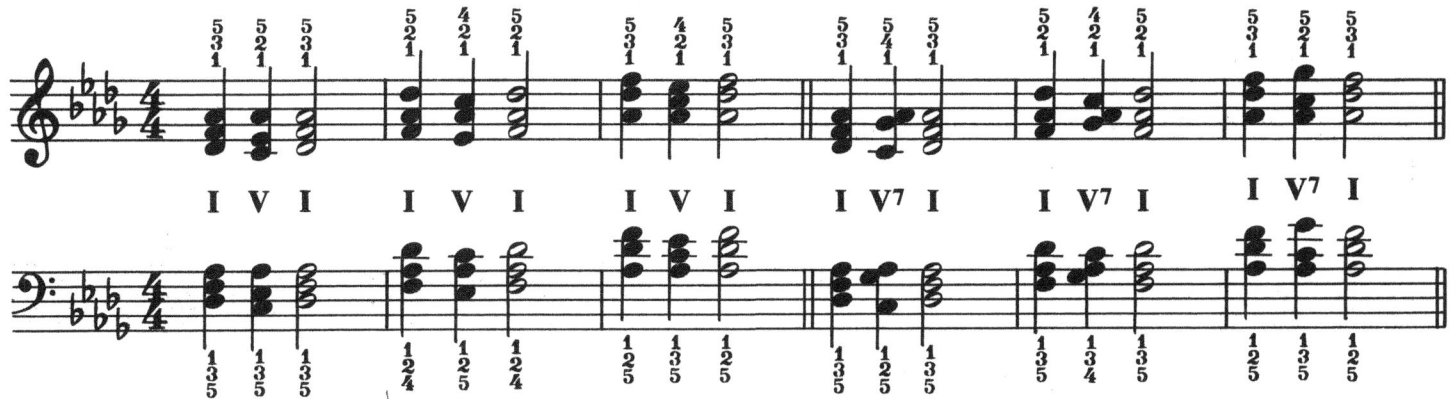

D♭ MINOR CADENCES (See C♯ minor cadences on page 23.)

A♭ MAJOR and G♯ MINOR — Scales & Triads

A♭ MAJOR SCALE in TETRACHORDS
Key Signature: 4 flats (B♭, E♭, A♭ & D♭).

A♭ MAJOR SCALE, ONE OCTAVE, hands separately or together

For the two-octave scale, see page 45.

G♯ HARMONIC MINOR SCALE, hands separately or together
G♯ Minor is the Relative Minor of B MAJOR. Key Signature: 5 sharps (F♯, C♯, G♯, D♯ & A♯).
The 7th scale tone (F♯) is raised one half-step ascending and descending.

For the two-octave scale, see page 48.

TRIADS in 3 POSITIONS, hands separately or together

A♭ MAJOR TRIAD   G♯ MINOR TRIAD

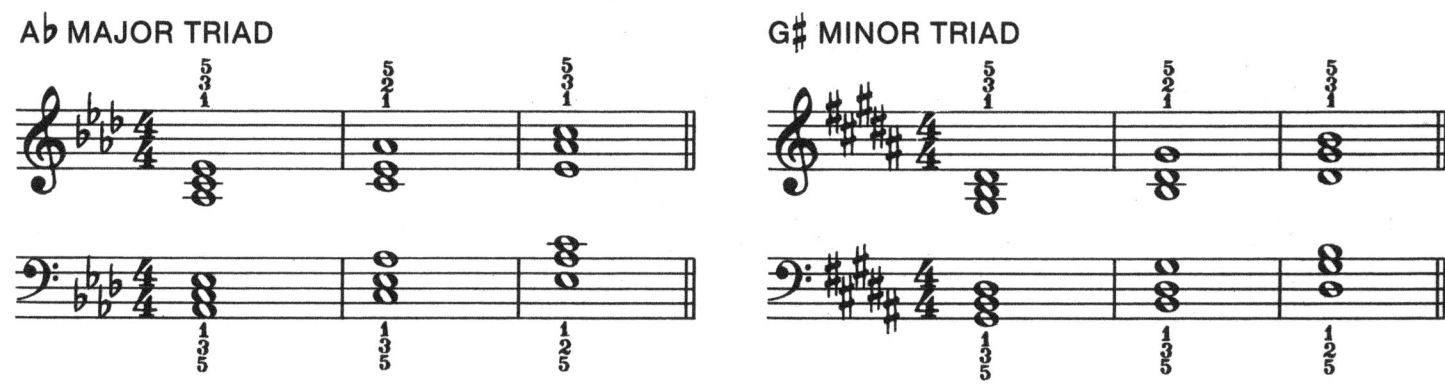

Arpeggios & Cadences

A♭ MAJOR ARPEGGIO
2nd time BOTH HANDS 2 octaves higher

G♯ MINOR ARPEGGIO
2nd time BOTH HANDS 2 octaves higher

A♭ MAJOR ARPEGGIO, with thumb turns

G♯ MINOR ARPEGGIO, with thumb turns

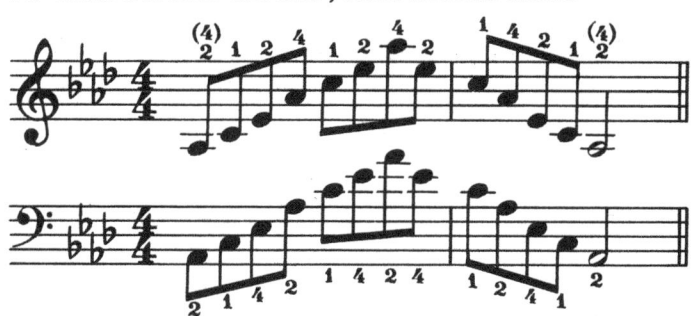

A♭ MAJOR CADENCES, hands separately or together

G♯ MINOR CADENCES, hands separately or together

E♭ MAJOR and E♭ MINOR — Scales & Triads

E♭ MAJOR SCALE in TETRACHORDS
Key Signature: 3 flats (B♭, E♭ & A♭).

E♭ MAJOR SCALE, ONE OCTAVE, hands separately or together

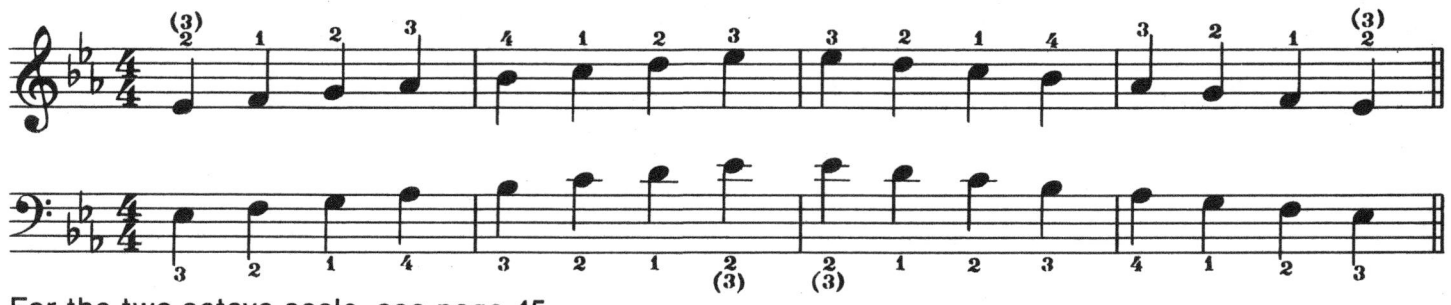

For the two-octave scale, see page 45.

E♭ HARMONIC MINOR SCALE, hands separately or together
E♭ Minor is the Relative Minor of G♭ MAJOR. Key Signature: 6 flats (B♭, E♭, A♭, D♭, G♭ & C♭).
The 7th scale tone (D♭) is raised one half-step ascending and descending.

For the two-octave scale, see page 48.

TRIADS in 3 POSITIONS, hands separately or together

E♭ MAJOR TRIAD   E♭ MINOR TRIAD

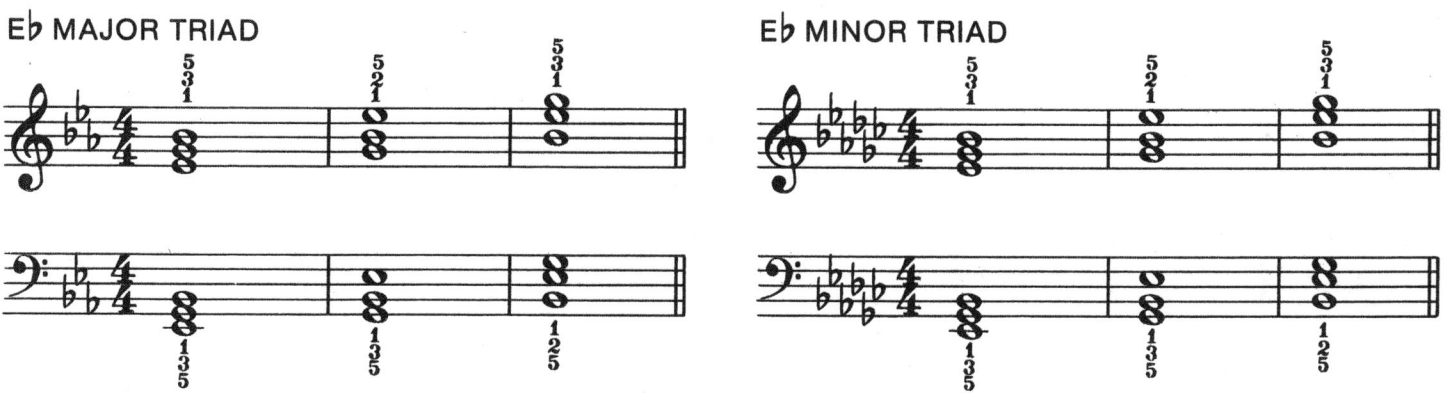

Arpeggios & Cadences

E♭ MAJOR ARPEGGIO
2nd time BOTH HANDS 2 octaves higher

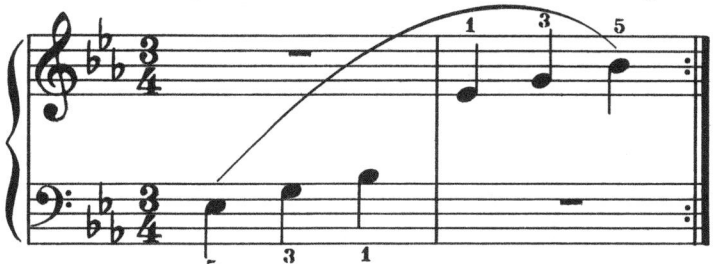

E♭ MINOR ARPEGGIO
2nd time BOTH HANDS 2 octaves higher

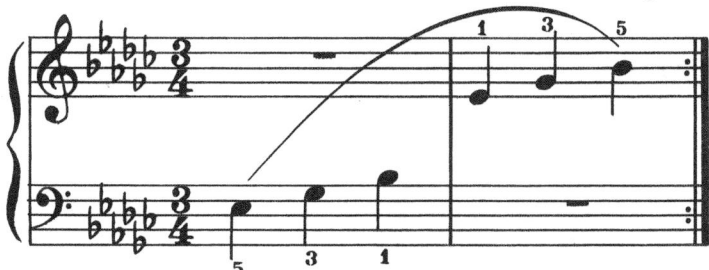

E♭ MAJOR ARPEGGIO, with thumb turns

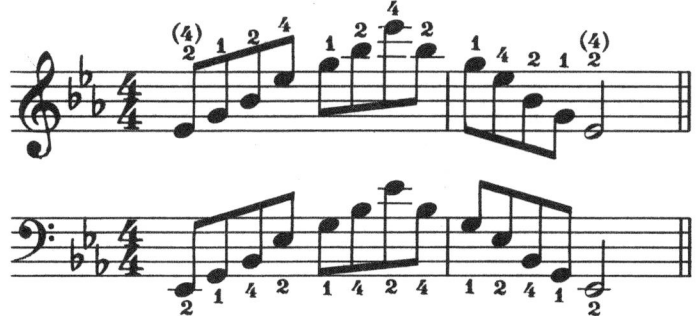

E♭ MINOR ARPEGGIO, with thumb turns

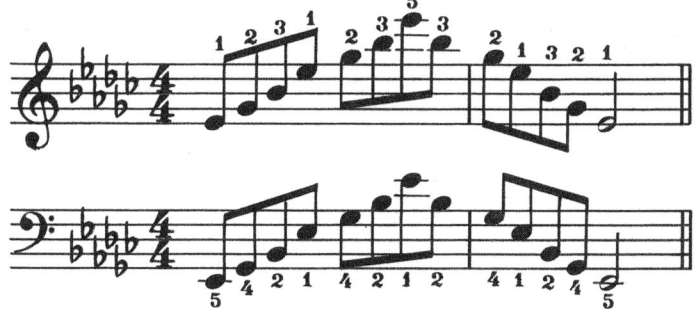

E♭ MAJOR CADENCES, hands separately or together

E♭ MINOR CADENCES, hands separately or together

B♭ MAJOR and B♭ MINOR — Scales & Triads

B♭ MAJOR SCALE in TETRACHORDS
Key Signature: 2 flats (B♭ & E♭).

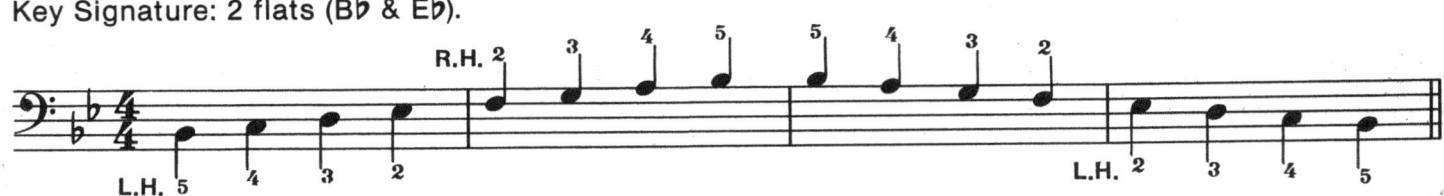

B♭ MAJOR SCALE, ONE OCTAVE, hands separately or together

For the two-octave scale, see page 45.

B♭ HARMONIC MINOR SCALE, hands separately or together
B♭ Minor is the Relative Minor of D♭ MAJOR. Key Signature: 5 flats (B♭, E♭, A♭, D♭ & G♭).
The 7th scale tone (A♭) is raised one half-step ascending and descending.

For the two-octave scale, see page 48.

TRIADS in 3 POSITIONS, hands separately or together
B♭ MAJOR TRIAD   B♭ MINOR TRIAD

Arpeggios & Cadences

B♭ MAJOR ARPEGGIO
2nd time BOTH HANDS 2 octaves higher

B♭ MINOR ARPEGGIO
2nd time BOTH HANDS 2 octaves higher

B♭ MAJOR ARPEGGIO, with thumb turns

B♭ MINOR ARPEGGIO, with thumb turns

B♭ MAJOR CADENCES, hands separately or together

B♭ MINOR CADENCES, hands separately or together

F MAJOR and F MINOR — Scales & Triads

F MAJOR SCALE in TETRACHORDS
Key Signature: 1 flat (B♭).

F MAJOR SCALE, ONE OCTAVE, hands separately or together

For the two-octave scale, see page 45.

F HARMONIC MINOR SCALE, hands separately or together
F Minor is the Relative Minor of A♭ MAJOR. Key Signature: 4 flats (B♭, E♭, A♭ & D♭).
The 7th scale tone (E♭) is raised one half-step ascending and descending.

For the two-octave scale, see page 48.

TRIADS in 3 POSITIONS, hands separately or together

F MAJOR TRIAD   F MINOR TRIAD

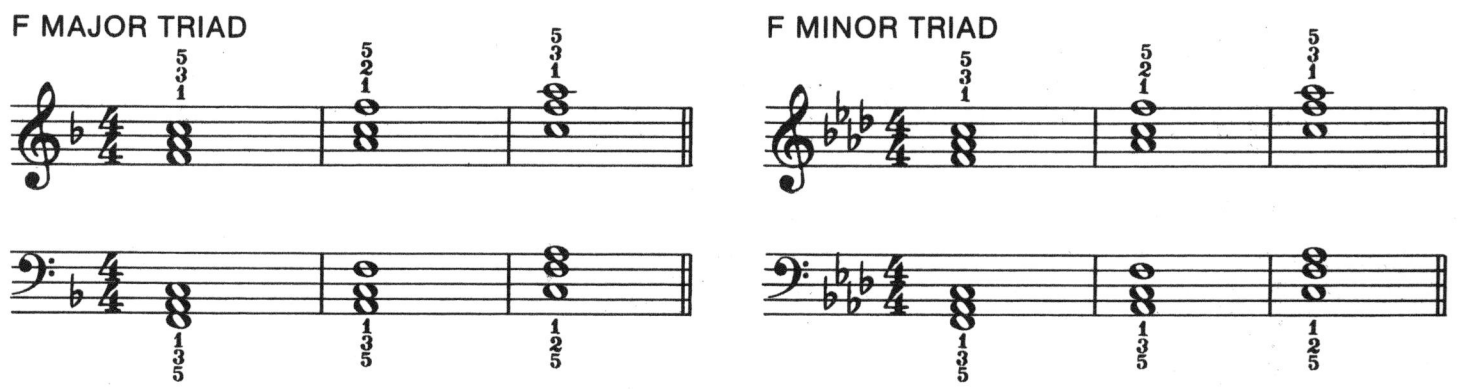

Arpeggios & Cadences

F MAJOR ARPEGGIO
2nd time BOTH HANDS 2 octaves higher

F MINOR ARPEGGIO
2nd time BOTH HANDS 2 octaves higher

F MAJOR ARPEGGIO, with thumb turns

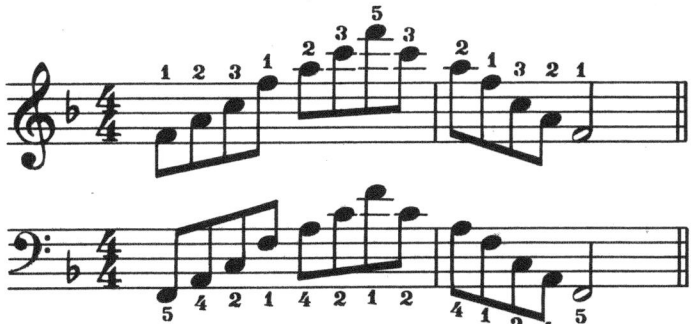

F MINOR ARPEGGIO, with thumb turns

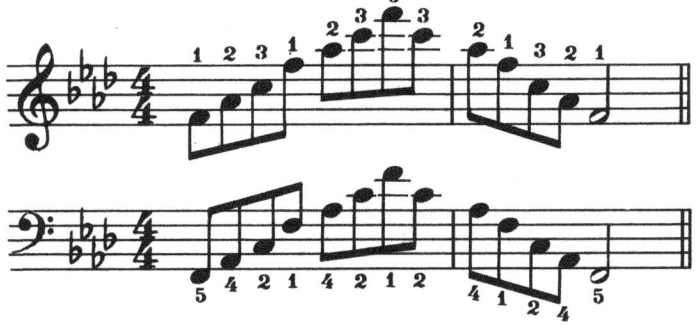

F MAJOR CADENCES, hands separately or together

F MINOR CADENCES, hands separately or together

Major Keys, Minor Keys & Key Signatures
Around the Circle of 5ths

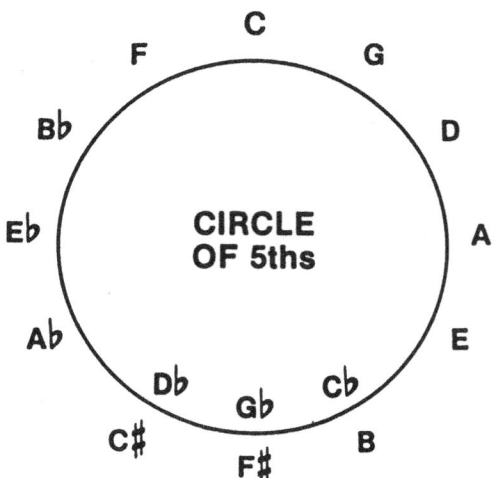

Beginning with F and moving clockwise around the Circle of 5ths, the order of keys is:

F C G D A E B F♯ C♯

Beginning with B♭ and moving counter-clockwise, the order of keys is:

B♭ E♭ A♭ D♭ G♭ C♭

The order in which SHARPS occur in key signatures is:

F♯ C♯ G♯ D♯ A♯ E♯ B♯

The order in which FLATS occur in key signatures is:

B♭ E♭ A♭ D♭ G♭ C♭ F♭

MAJOR KEY	RELATIVE MINOR KEY	KEY SIGNATURE	SHARPS OR FLATS IN KEY SIGNATURE						
C MAJOR	A MINOR	No ♯'s, no ♭'s							
G MAJOR	E MINOR	1♯	F♯						
D MAJOR	B MINOR	2♯'s	F♯	C♯					
A MAJOR	F♯ MINOR	3♯'s	F♯	C♯	G♯				
E MAJOR	C♯ MINOR	4♯'s	F♯	C♯	G♯	D♯			
B MAJOR	G♯ MINOR	5♯'s	F♯	C♯	G♯	D♯	A♯		
F♯ MAJOR	D♯ MINOR	6♯'s	F♯	C♯	G♯	D♯	A♯	E♯	
C♯ MAJOR	A♯ MINOR	7♯'s	F♯	C♯	G♯	D♯	A♯	E♯	B♯
F MAJOR	D MINOR	1♭	B♭						
B♭ MAJOR	G MINOR	2♭'s	B♭	E♭					
E♭ MAJOR	C MINOR	3♭'s	B♭	E♭	A♭				
A♭ MAJOR	F MINOR	4♭'s	B♭	E♭	A♭	D♭			
D♭ MAJOR	B♭ MINOR	5♭'s	B♭	E♭	A♭	D♭	G♭		
G♭ MAJOR	E♭ MINOR	6♭'s	B♭	E♭	A♭	D♭	G♭	C♭	
C♭ MAJOR	A♭ MINOR	7♭'s	B♭	E♭	A♭	D♭	G♭	C♭	F♭

Enrichment Options

Any of the following options may be used with the major and minor keys.
The teacher will assign specific options in keys the student is currently practicing.

CADENCES, root in bass **CADENCES, root in soprano**

HARMONIZING THE SCALE, chords in bass

HARMONIZING THE SCALE, chords in treble

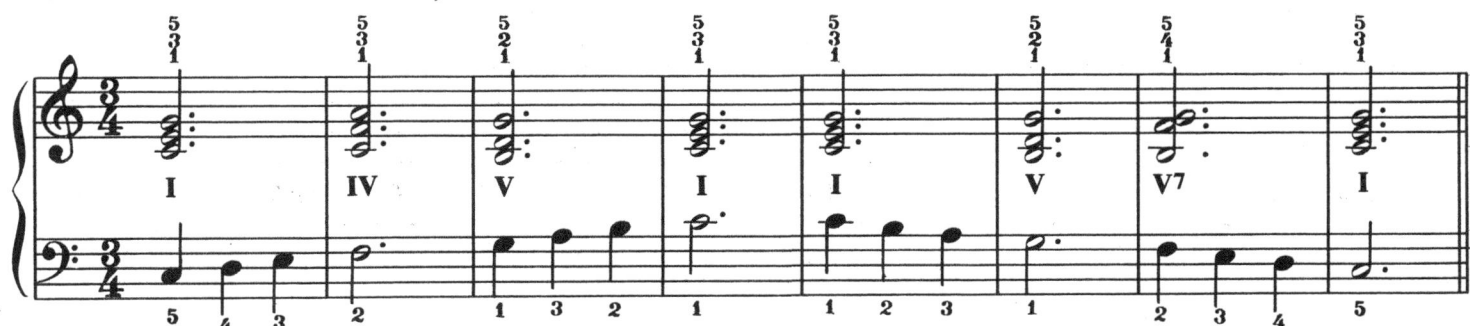

SCALE, both hands staccato

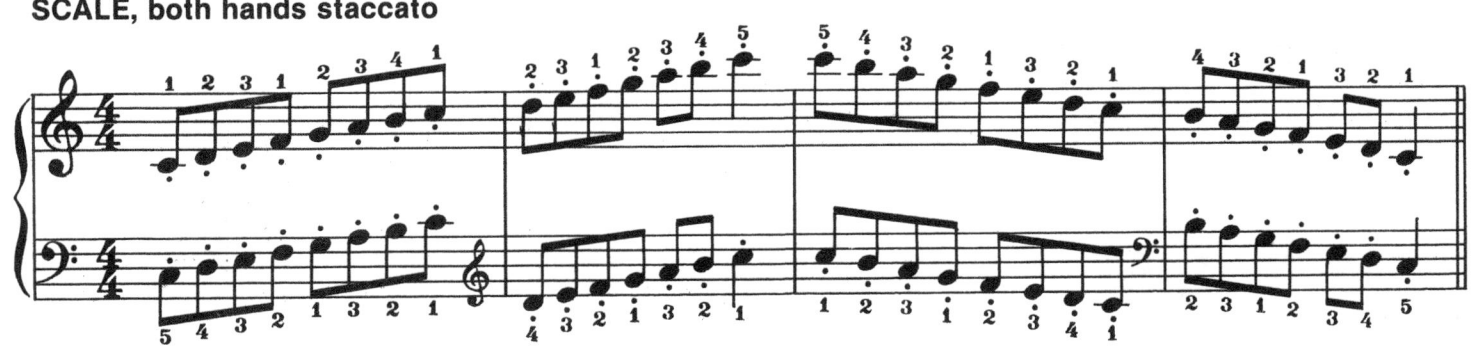

SCALE, right hand staccato, left hand legato

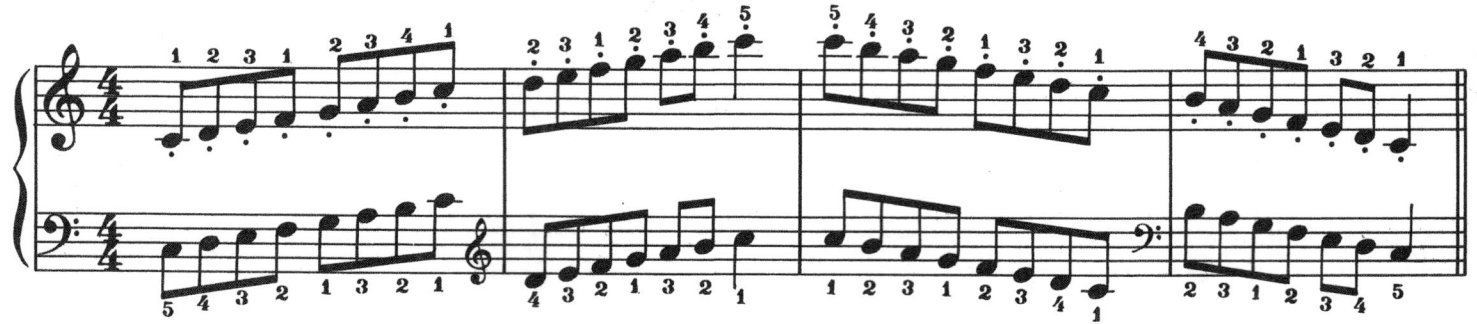

SCALE, right hand legato, left hand staccato

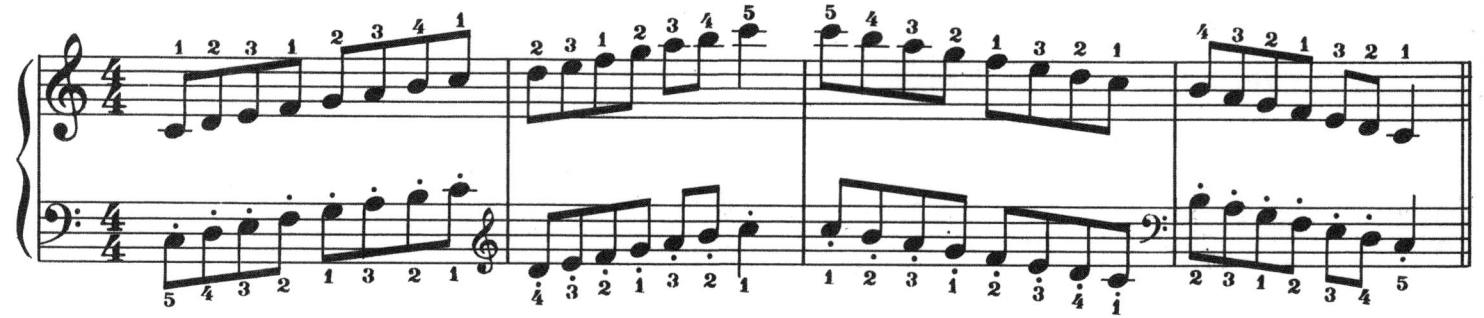

SCALE, 16th notes

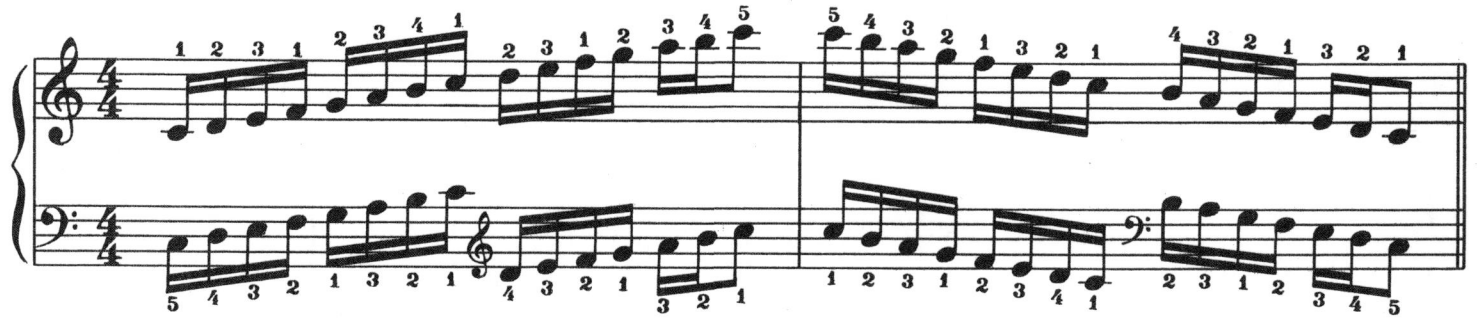

SCALE, dotted 8th followed by 16th note rhythm

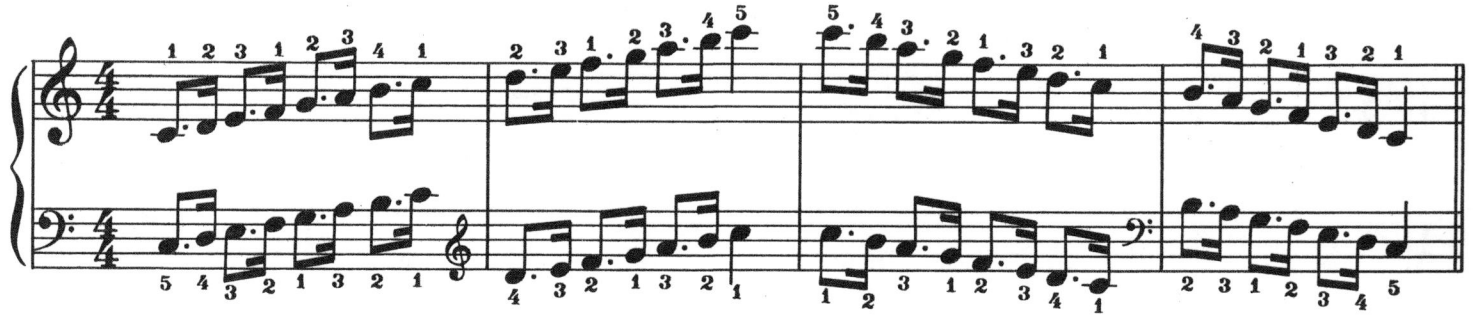

Triad Chain

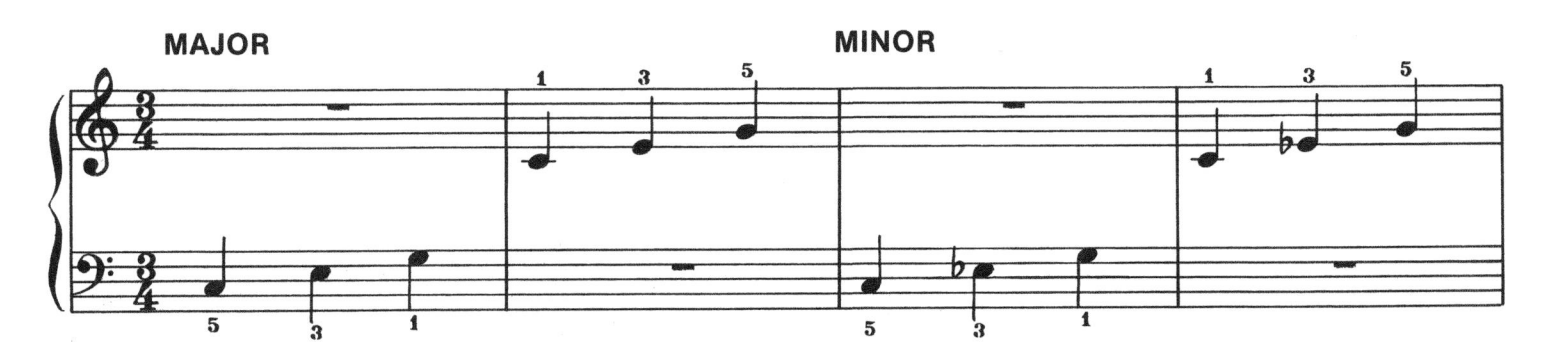

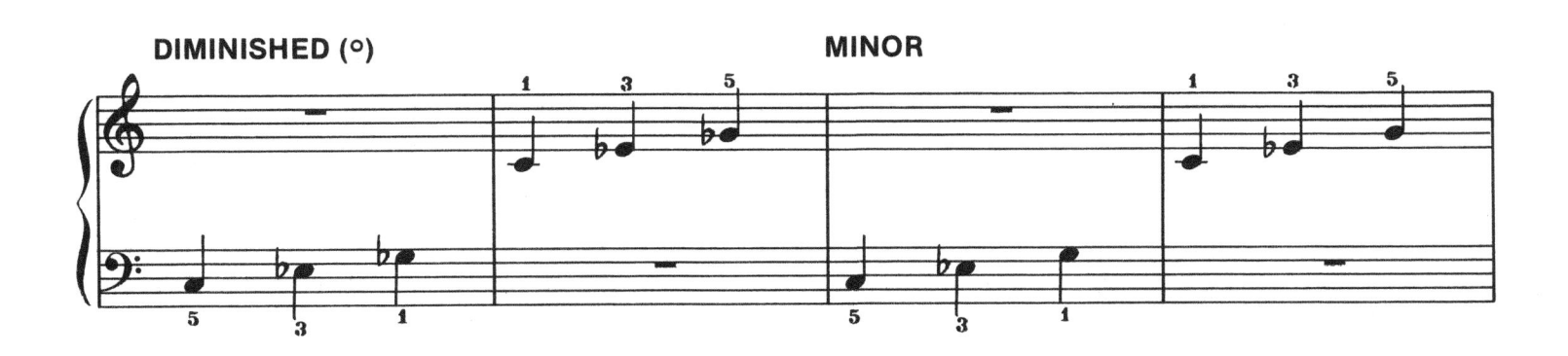

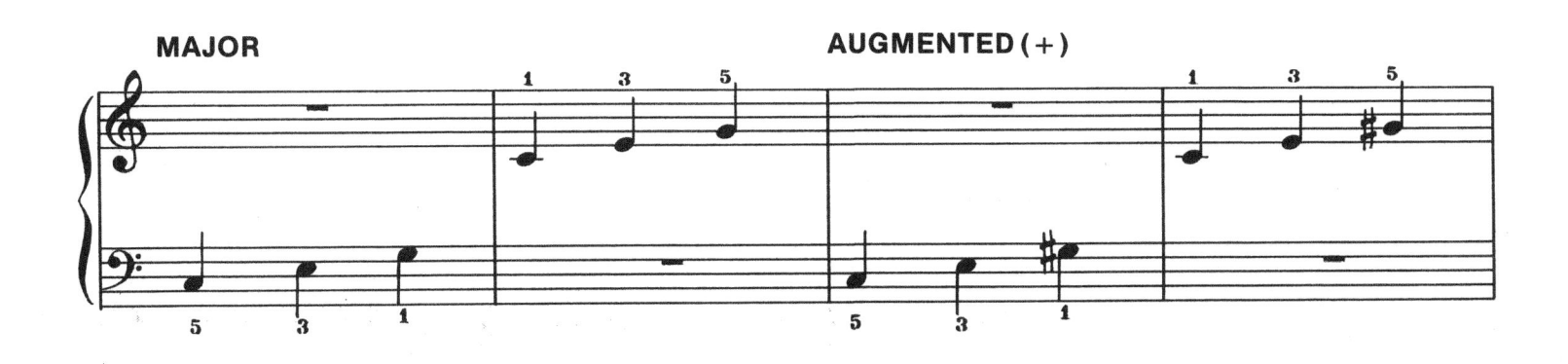

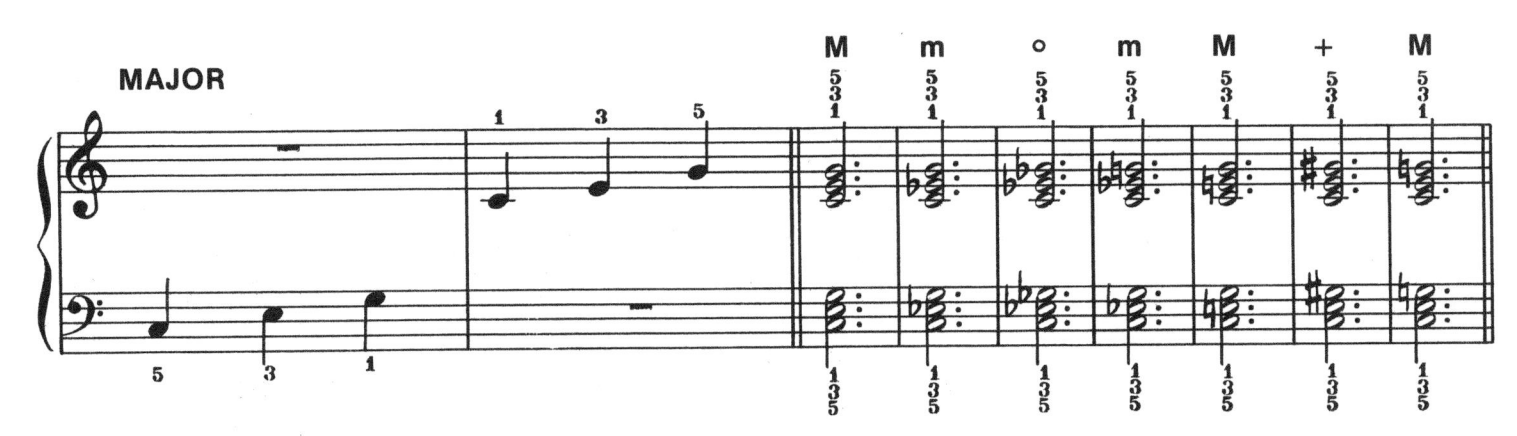

Play the triad chain starting on every tonic major triad.

Dominant Seventh Chord (V⁷) resolving to its Major Tonic Chord (I)

KEY OF F MAJOR

KEY OF B♭ MAJOR

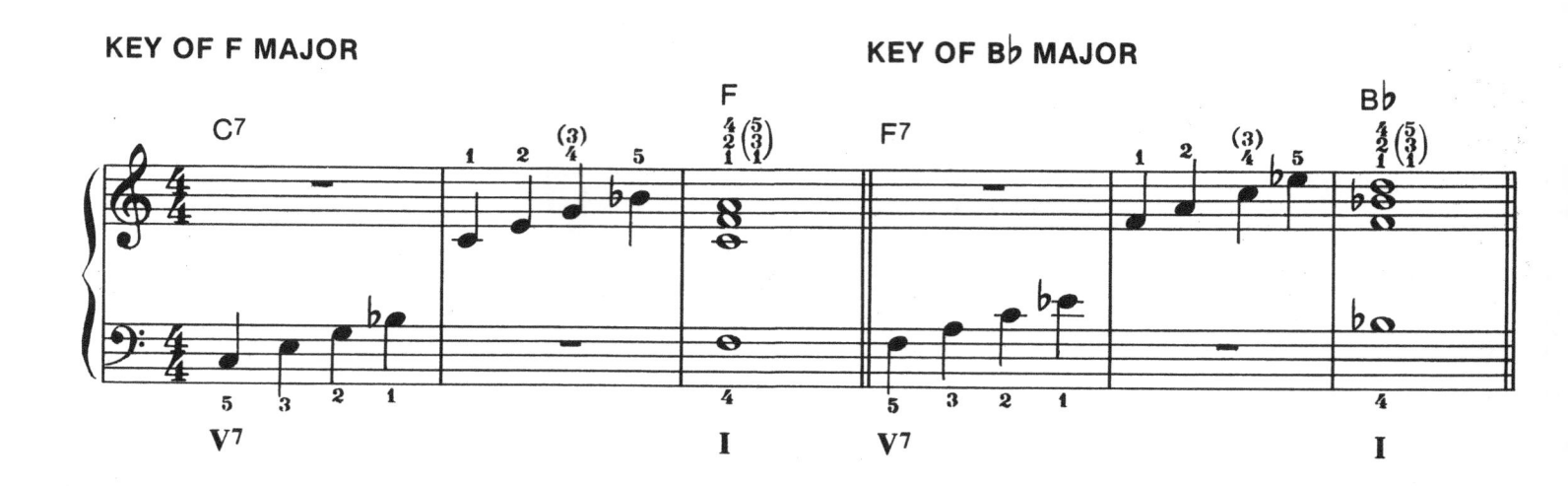

KEY OF E♭ MAJOR

KEY OF A♭ MAJOR

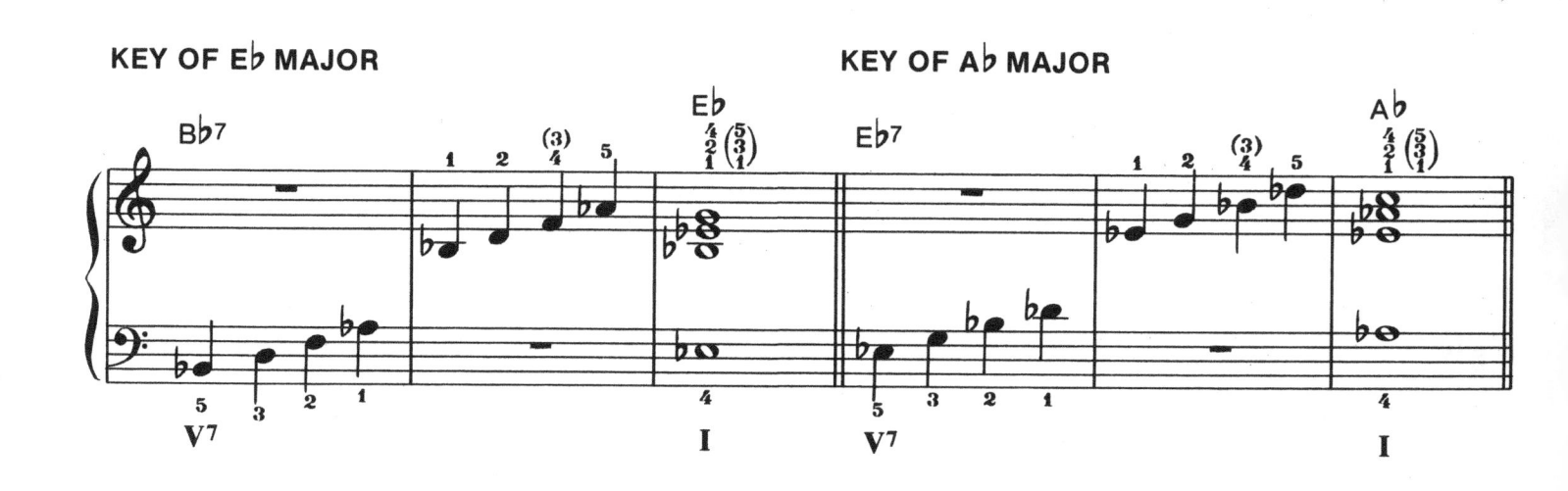

KEY OF D♭ MAJOR

KEY OF G♭ MAJOR

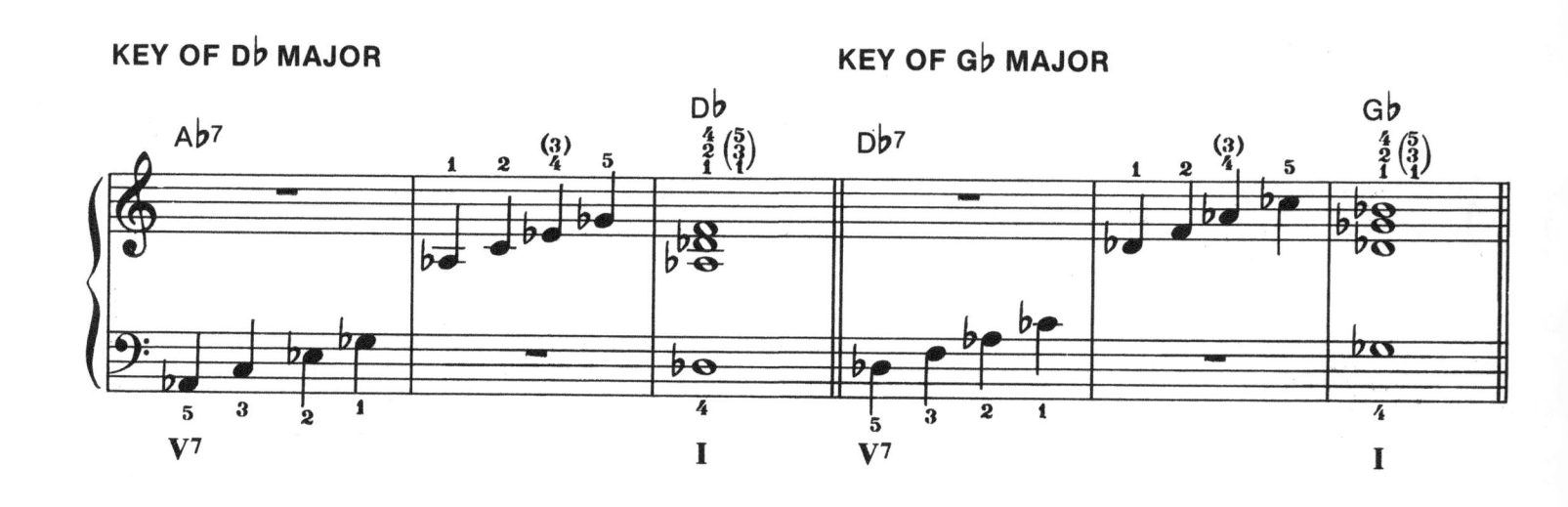

KEY OF F♯ MAJOR **KEY OF B MAJOR**

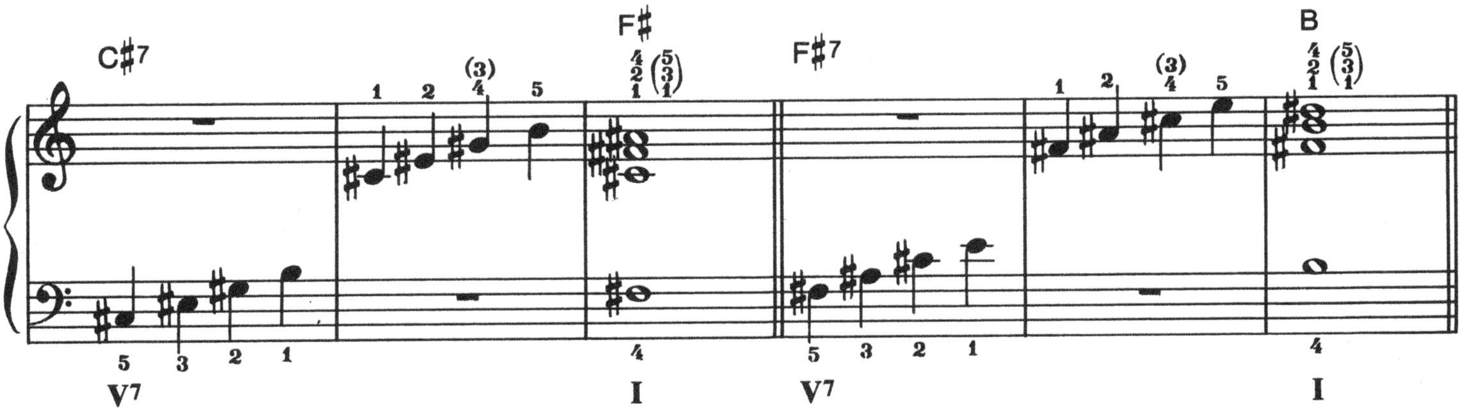

KEY OF E MAJOR **KEY OF A MAJOR**

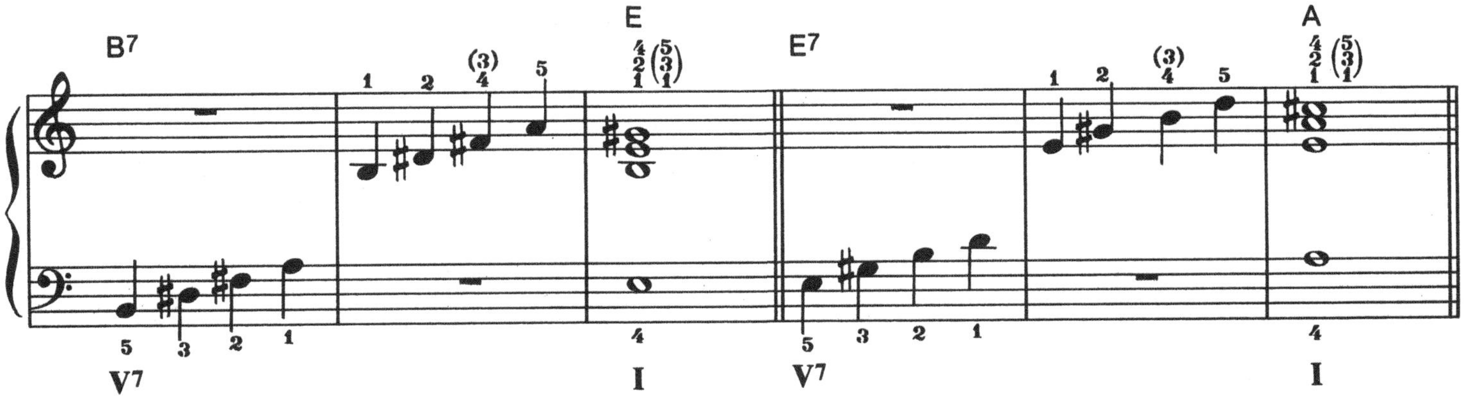

KEY OF D MAJOR **KEY OF G MAJOR** **KEY OF C MAJOR**

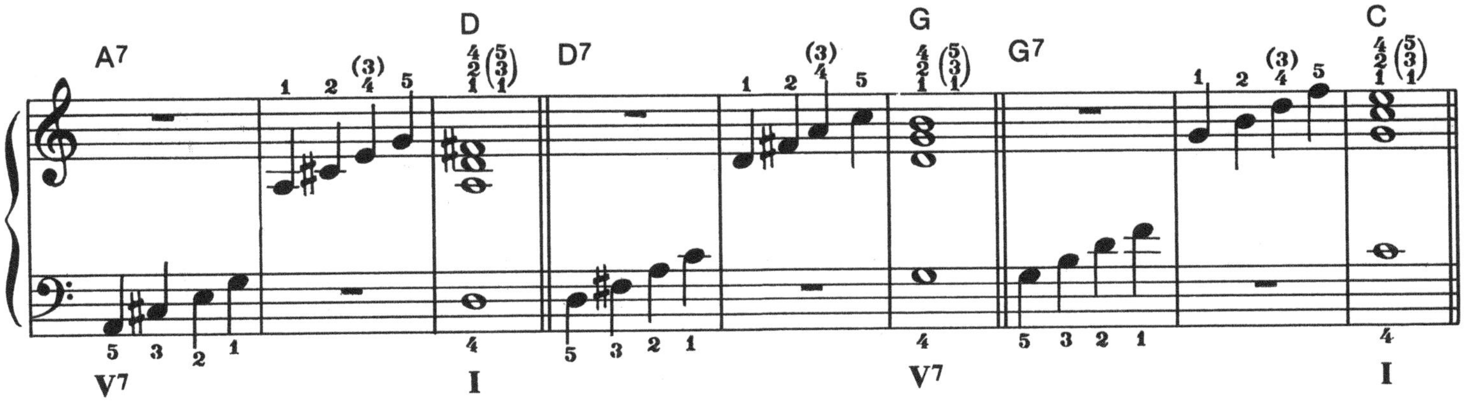

Dominant Seventh Chord (V⁷) resolving to its Minor Tonic Chord (i)

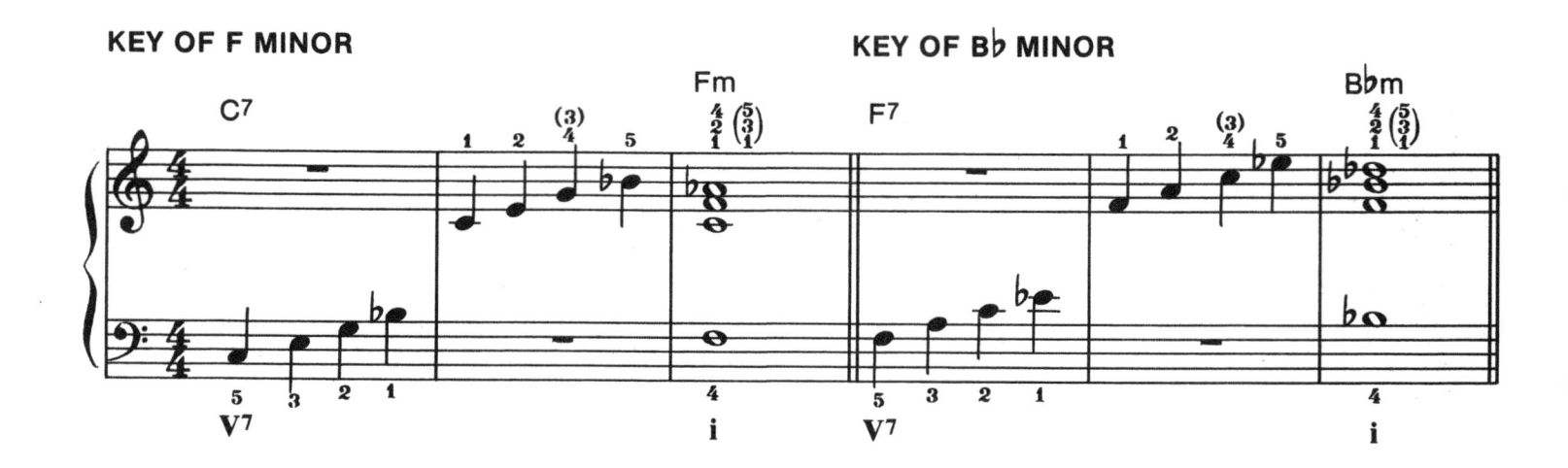

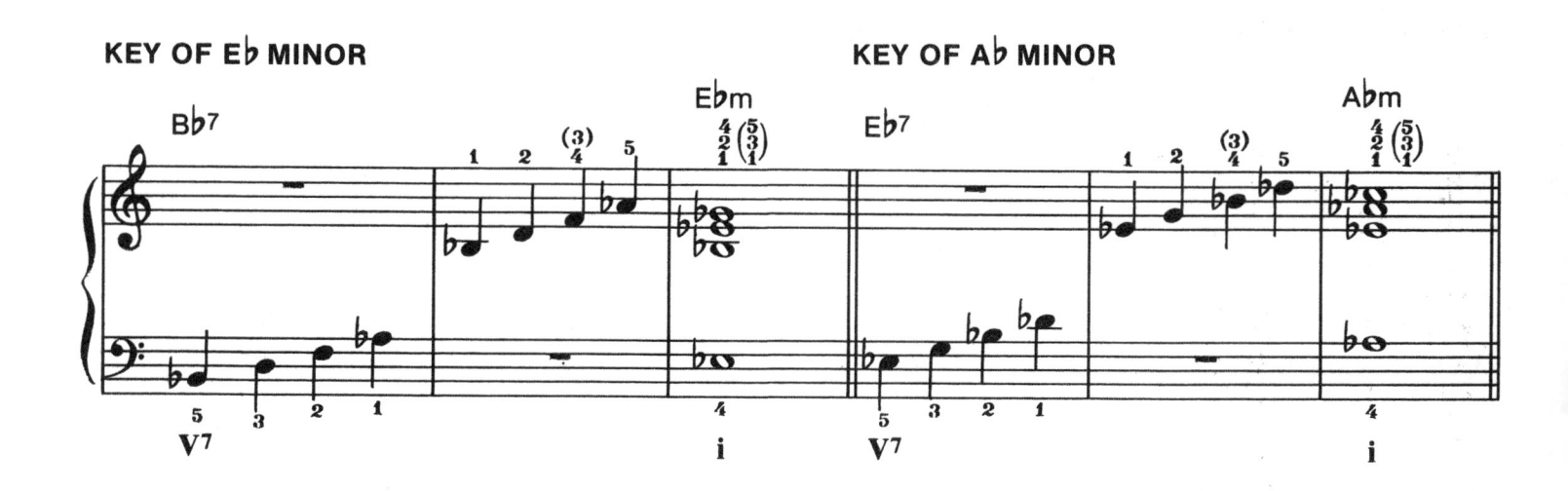

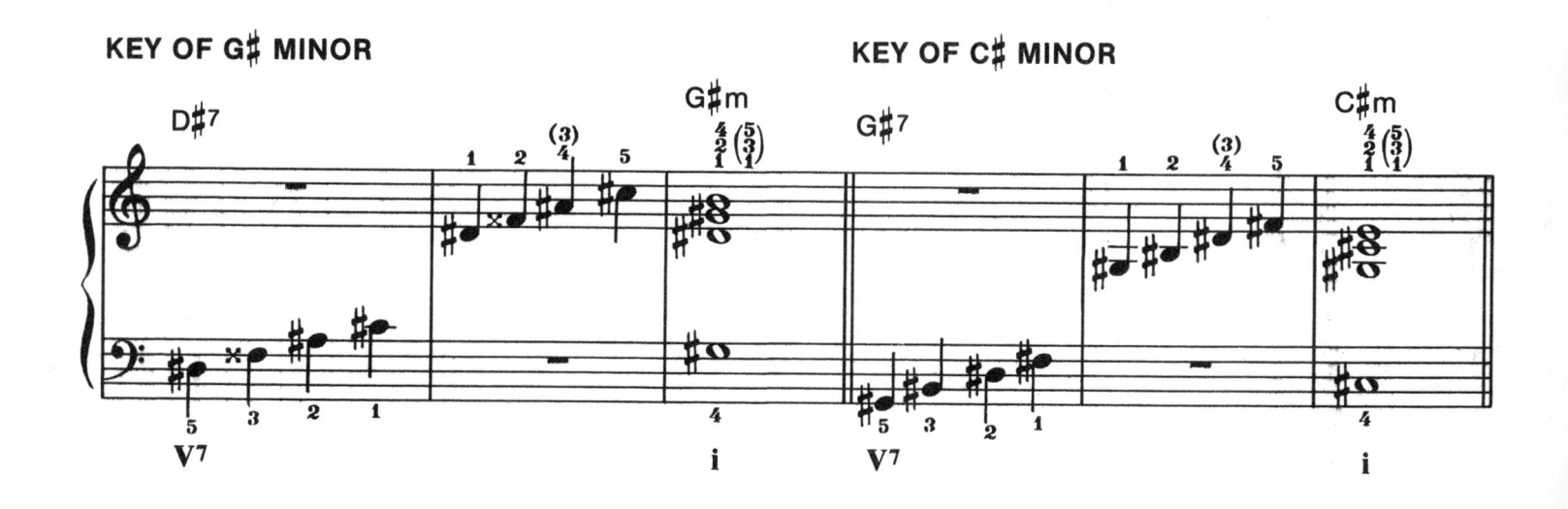

KEY OF F MINOR

KEY OF B♭ MINOR

KEY OF E♭ MINOR

KEY OF A♭ MINOR

KEY OF G♯ MINOR

KEY OF C♯ MINOR

KEY OF G♭ MINOR **KEY OF F♯ MINOR**

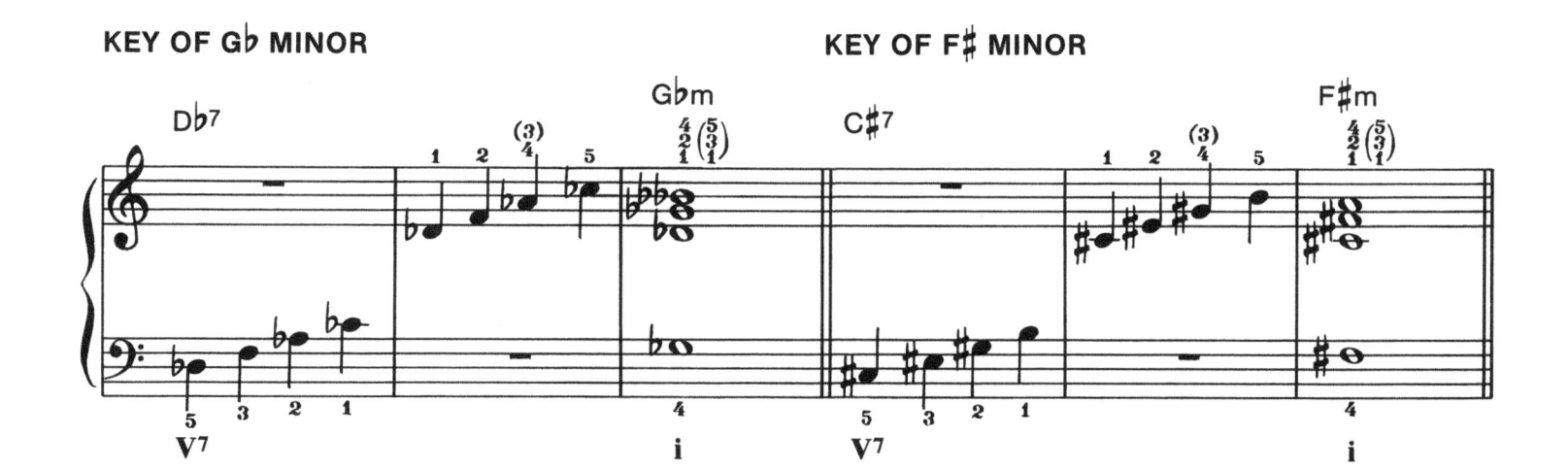

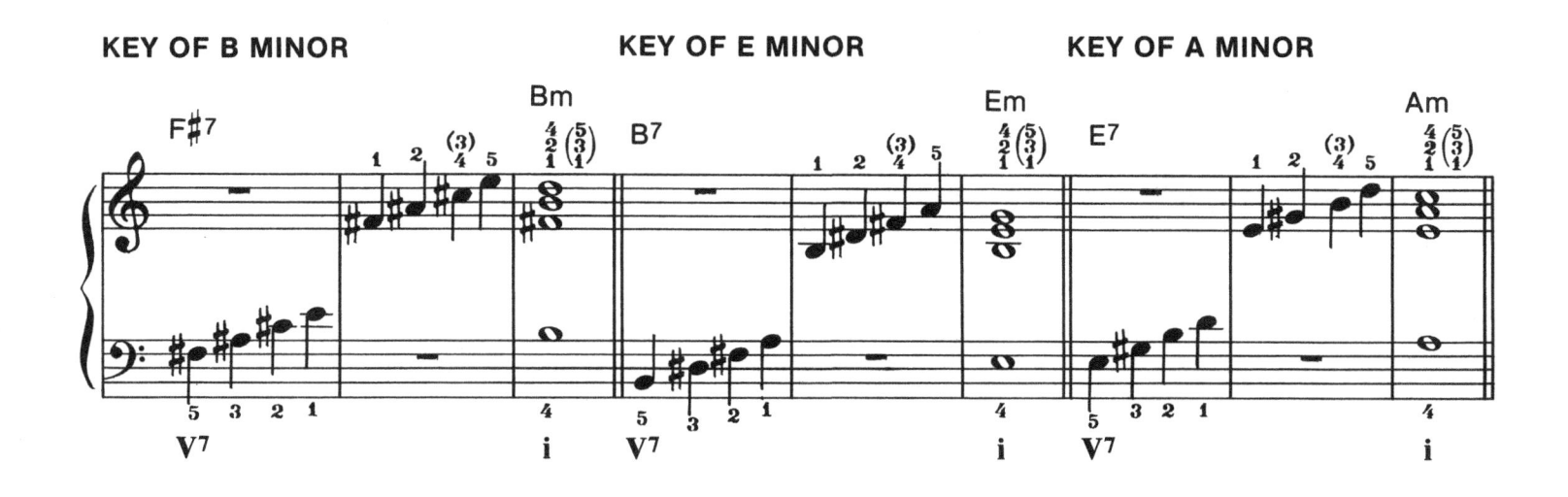

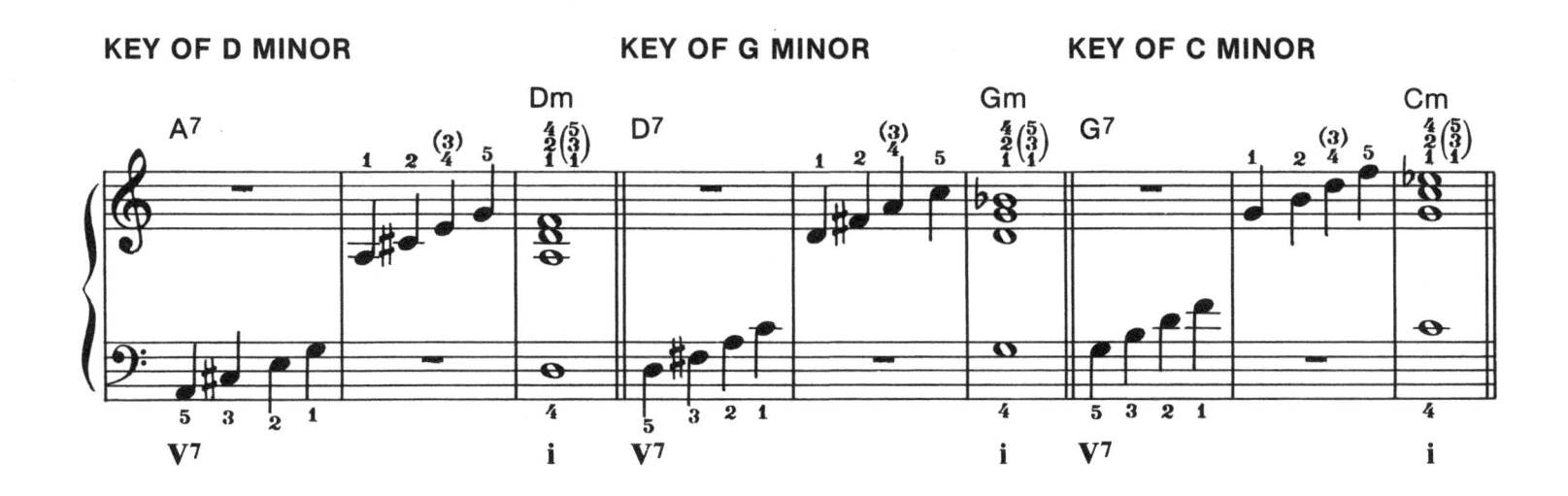

KEY OF B MINOR **KEY OF E MINOR** **KEY OF A MINOR**

KEY OF D MINOR **KEY OF G MINOR** **KEY OF C MINOR**

Scales—The Grand Form

The following SCALE ROUTINE is used by many piano conservatories and master piano teachers throughout the world. It may be used with all the major and minor scales that follow.

Major Scales, 2 Octaves

C MAJOR

G MAJOR

D MAJOR

A MAJOR

E MAJOR

B MAJOR

C♭ MAJOR

F♯ MAJOR

G♭ MAJOR

C♯ MAJOR

D♭ MAJOR

A♭ MAJOR

E♭ MAJOR

B♭ MAJOR

F MAJOR

Harmonic Minor Scales, 2 Octaves

C MINOR

G MINOR

D MINOR

A MINOR

47

E MINOR

B MINOR

F♯ MINOR

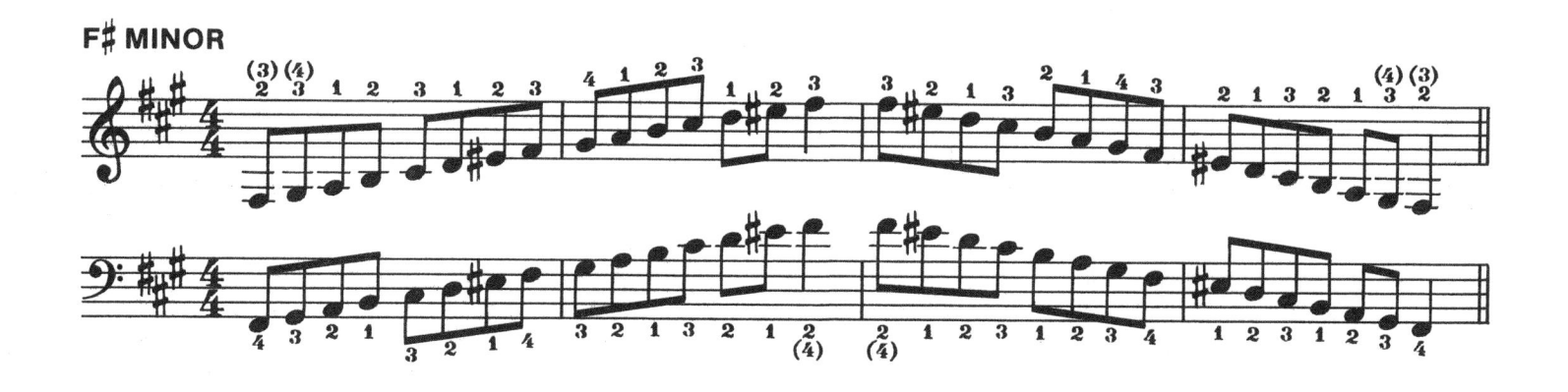

C♯ MINOR

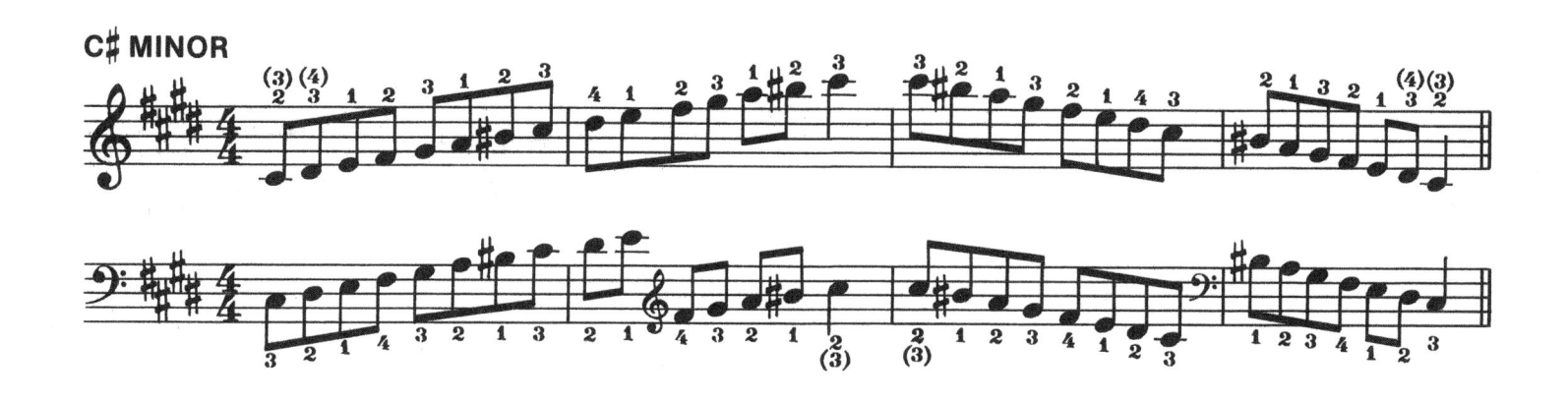

G♯ MINOR

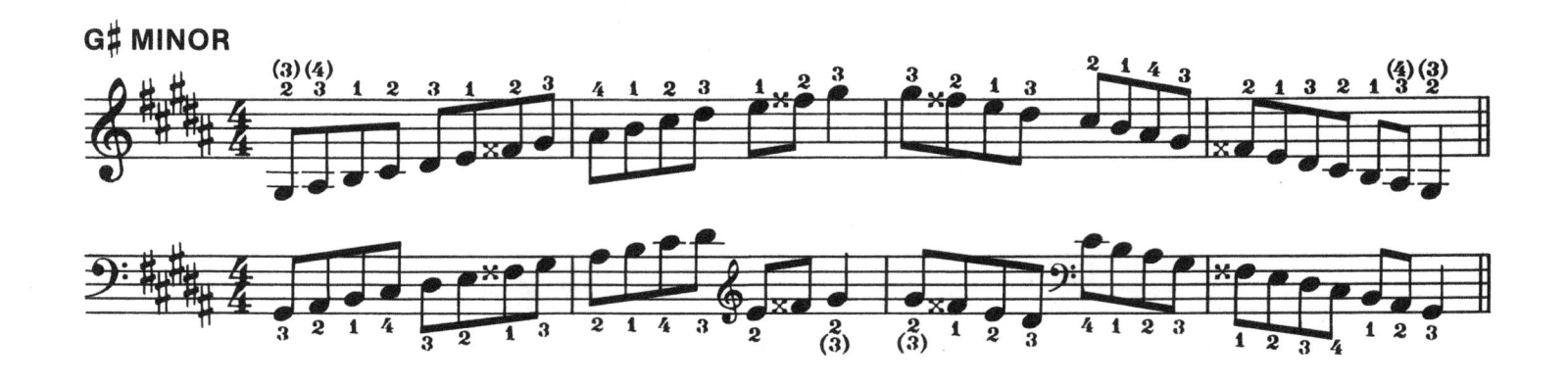

E♭ MINOR

B♭ MINOR

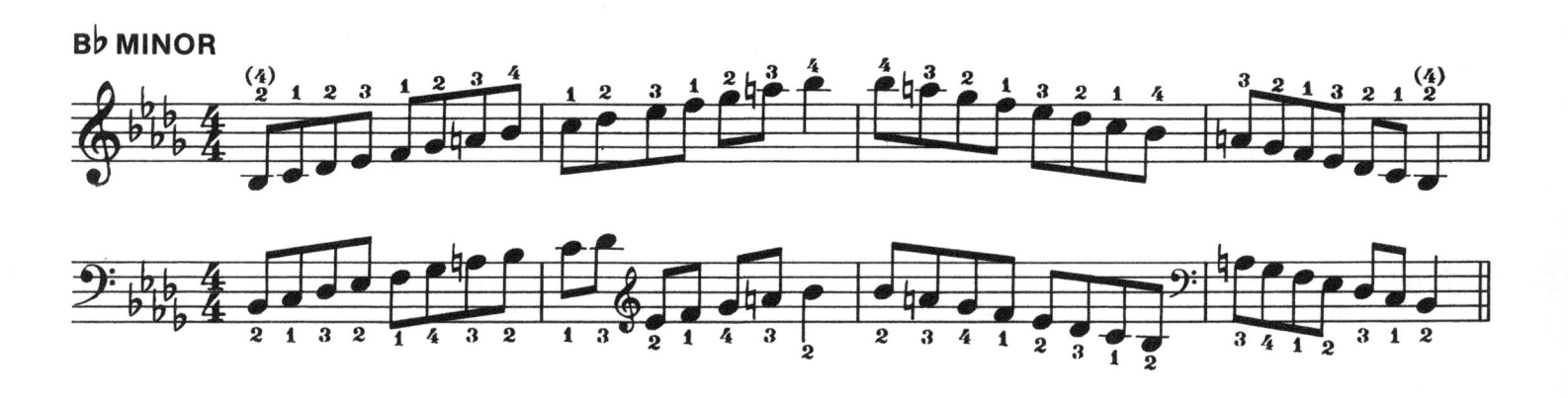

F MINOR